Brighton and Hove

Brighton's most popular

Anne of Cleves House	8	Lewes Bonfire Celebration	25
Brighton Art Fair	9	Lewes Castle	26
Brighton Artists' Open House	10	London to Brighton Mini Run	27
Brighton Festival & Fringe	12	London to Brighton	
Brighton Marina	14	Veteran Car Run	28
Brighton Pier	15	North Laine	30
Brighton Seafront	16	Preston Manor	32
Burning the Clocks	18	Royal Pavilion	34
Charleston	20	Sea Life Centre	36
Devil's Dyke	22	Volk's Railway	37
The Lanes	24	West Pier Ruins	38

Other major attractions 40-41

Architecture, Heritage and Galleries 42-49

Entertainment 50-57

Theatre and Comedy	50-51	Live Music	53-54
Cinemas	52	Night Clubs	55-57

Eating and Drinking 58-67

Cafés	58-59	Seafood, Fish	
Pubs/Bars	59-61	(and Chips) Restaurants	64-65
British Restaurants	61-62	Vegetarian and	
European Restaurants	62-63	Vegan Restaurants	65-67
African, American			
and Asian Restaurants	63-64		

Shopping 68-75

Brighton's Villages 76-81

Gay Brighton and Hove 82-84

Gardens 86-95

Walking 96-103

Where to Stay 104-106

Hotels	104	B&B and Guest Houses	104

Other useful information 107-109

Map	107-109	Travel Information	110-111

4
Brighton and Hove

Colourful, vibrant and endearingly eccentric, Brighton and Hove has long been one of the UK's most celebrated visitor destinations. Its coastal location makes it a popular choice for traditional family summer outings, while its dazzling variety of galleries, designer boutiques, restaurants and places to stay – from cosy seafront guesthouses to chic hotels – have won it a growing reputation as a stylish, cosmopolitan city and a desirable romantic getaway.

Cosmopolitan character
However, this unique city has many other strings to its bow, ensuring its appeal is far from just seasonal. Granted city status by HM the Queen in 2000, what were the 'twin towns' of Brighton and Hove currently have a joint population of less than 250,000. Yet, while this modest size lends the place an intimate 'village-like' feel, and it is possible to walk from one end to the other in a fraction of the time it would take to cross larger cities, its cosmopolitan character, adventurous spirit and wealth of attractions have earned it big-city popularity.

Over the centuries
According to historical records, Brighton began life as a small Anglo-Saxon settlement in the sixth century, later growing into a sizeable village under the name Brighthelmstone. Though occupied continuously throughout the Medieval era, it was in the 18th century that it underwent its first sustained period of expansion.

5
Brighton and Hove

Regency splendour
In 1750, Brighton became fashionable almost overnight when Dr Richard Russell (soon known as 'Dr Brighton') began popularising his belief in the healing qualities of seawater, promoting the then medium-sized fishing port as a model spa. Intrigued tourists started to trickle in, but it was only after a visit by George, Prince of Wales, in 1783 that the influx began. Within 30 years, Brighton had become a flourishing resort; location of the Royal Pavilion, pleasure palace for the Prince Regent (as George was by then); and a home from home for gentry who acquired lavish townhouses in the panoramic Regency squares and crescents of Brunswick and Kemp Town.

Diverse riches
Today, Brighton and Hove continue to retain this early glamour, while constantly gaining new layers of richness and diversity. It boasts one of Britain's largest gay communities and a growing number of immigrants from Europe, Africa and the Far East – and each year attracts eight million tourists from around the world. Whether you're after a weekend of sight-seeing, an indulgent pre-Christmas shopping spree or a night of feverish clubbing, this 21st-century city is guaranteed to have something for you.

6
Brighton and Hove

Want More Information?
For accommodation information and availability, and information on special offers:
Visit www.visitbrighton.com,
Brighton's official tourism website

When you're here visit the Information Centre for help with:
- local and national accommodation bookings
- coach and tour bus tickets
- attraction and theatre tickets
- guides and souvenirs

7 Brighton and Hove

Or call: 09067112255 (calls cost 50p per minute)
Or email: brighton-tourism@brighton-hove.gov.uk

Brighton & Hove Visitor Centre,
The Royal Pavilion Shop,
4/5 Pavilion Buildings,
Brighton BN1 1EE

VisitBrighton is the official tourism organisation for Brighton and Hove.

8
Anne of Cleves House

www.visitbrighton.com

This handsome Tudor timber-framed house purportedly formed part of the 1541 divorce settlement between Henry VIII and his fourth wife, Anne of Cleves. Situated in the historic East Sussex county town of Lewes, a 20-minute drive from Brighton, it is both a popular tourist attraction and an oft-requested wedding venue.

Southover High Street, Lewes BN7 1JA

T (01273) 474610

www.sussexpast.co.uk

March to October: Tues-Sat 10-5, Sun, Mon & Bank Holidays 11-5. Nov to Feb: Tues-Sat 10-5. Closed Christmas.

Museum
With its angled beams and low ceilings, this charming 16th-century building is the perfect place to while away a leisurely afternoon. Its central focus is Lewes Folk Museum, which traces the town's history from the 1500s to the present day, displaying an extensive collection of Sussex crafts, ranging from traditional pottery through sculptured stonework from Lewes Priory (demolished during Henry's Dissolution of the Monasteries) to iron boot-scrapers and cannon.

Period Features
Among the building's most notable architectural features are the original leaded windows and magnificent Elizabethan fireplace in its elegant East Room, which is licensed for civil weddings. The house also boasts a beautiful walled garden.

Venue for Hire
Hiring the house for a wedding costs £375 (excluding registrar's fee), while receptions (up to 9pm) cost £50 an hour. It also hosts periodic themed events, including storytelling and ghost nights.

Prices
£3.50 adult (£3 OAP/student) £1.60 child, £8 family (two adults, two children), £6.50 family (one adult, four children), £1.60 disabled and carer. Joint tickets for the house and Lewes Castle are available.

★ Highlights
Impressive Tudor architecture
Lewes Folk Museum

i Information
♿ Limited

notable architectural features

0906 711 2255*

9
Brighton Art Fair

Now in its fourth year (2007), Brighton Art Fair is fast becoming one of the biggest and most talked-about annual events in the city's calendar.

i Brighton Corn Exchange, BN1 1UE
T (01273) 709709
www.brightonartfair.co.uk

❋ Last weekend in September Friday 10-7.30, Saturday and Sunday 10-6

Affordable Art

Shifted from a pre-Christmas slot to late September last year to make room for a sister event, in the shape of a winter craft fair, BAF (as it has come to be known) was the brainchild of printmakers and artists Sarah Young and Tessa Walliman. It aims to provide a commercial showcase for locally based artists and offer browsers a chance to obtain original artwork at highly competitive prices. As with London's popular Affordable Art Fair, the emphasis is on accessibility over pretension, with colourful prints and postcards being sold alongside the originals. The latter tend to go for anything between £50 and £1,500 – but rarely much more.

Popular with Artists

Though artists pay £500 to exhibit at the three-day event, there is never any shortage of applicants. In fact, it's so over-subscribed stands have to be rationed, with the organisers forced to choose out of 300-plus hopefuls.

Impressive Setting

Housed in the glorious hall of Brighton's historic Corn Exchange building, next door to the main city museum, BAF attracts more than 5,000 art lovers a year, providing a source of inspiration for Christmas bargain hunters and culture vultures alike.

★ Highlights
Quality, affordable original artwork for sale
Chance to meet artists
Historic venue

i Information
🍽 Bar
♿ Good
£ £5

*calls cost 50p per minute, UK only

10 Brighton Artists' Open Houses

www.visitbrighton.com

Brighton and Hove has long enjoyed an arty reputation, and this is seldom more manifest than in its regular 'open house' exhibitions, which take place not only in galleries and studios but also individuals' homes.

- *i* Throughout the city
- **T** (07783) 985358
- www.aoh.org.uk

- ❊ First four weekends in May. Times vary

Artists in Residence
Since 1982, groups of artists have collaborated to display their work in each other's halls and living rooms at weekends during the annual Brighton Festival, and most of the city's districts now boast their own 'art trails'. One of the longest established is run by the Fiveways Artists' Group, which currently comprises 16 painters and sculptors living in the Preston Park area. Among the newest is the Central Brighton Artists trail, which boasts 12 venues, including studios and shops in North Laine.

Expansion
Such is the trails' popularity that they are now being mimicked by other towns, and some areas of Brighton and Hove, notably Hanover, have begun to stage them in the run-up to Christmas, as well as May. Among the well-known names to have exhibited in open houses are Steve Bell, the Guardian cartoonist, and John Cake and Darren Neave, better known as The Little Artists, whose miniature Lego versions of work by the likes of Tracey Emin and Damien Hirst were shown at the 2006 festival.

★ Highlights
Biggest free art fair in Britain
Original artwork on sale at affordable prices
Chance to meet artists

i Information
♿ Good to limited
£ Free

regular 'open house' exhibitions

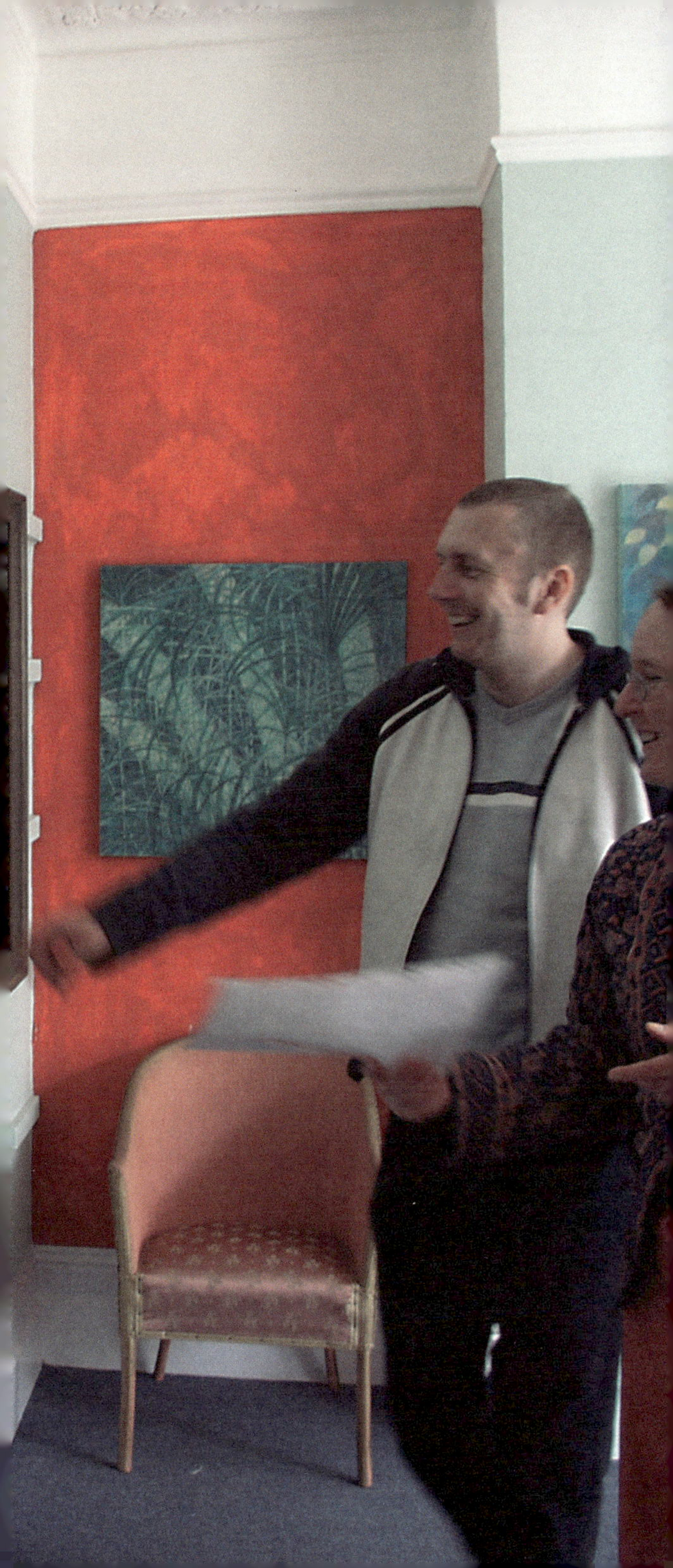

12
Brighton Festival & Fringe

www.visitbrighton.com

Brighton is home to the biggest arts festival in England – and Britain's second largest, after Edinburgh. In 2005, the annual three-week extravaganza marked its 40th anniversary, with record attendances of more than 500,000 across 200 mainstream festival and 500 fringe events.

- *i* Venues throughout city
- T (01273) 709709
  www.brightonfestival.org
- Throughout May. Times of events vary

Global Showcase

Since its humble beginnings, the Brighton Festival has evolved into a mammoth showcase for cutting-edge performers from the worlds of theatre, music and dance, and leading names in fine art, film and literature. As in Edinburgh, the festival now encompasses a variety of discrete strands, with brochures dedicated to everything from artists' open houses to book readings and other literary events.

Street Celebrations

Each May, the festival opens with a children's parade, in which thousands of youngsters march through the city centre, dressed as clowns, farm animals and cartoon characters, to the thumping rhythm of a samba band. Other highlights include the wacky Streets of Brighton programme – a series of free outdoor performances by artistes from around the world, ranging from stilt-walkers through fire-eaters to giant puppets. In recent years, the festival has culminated in the Big Splash – a dazzling firework display at Brighton Marina at dusk on the Sunday of its final weekend.

★ Highlights
England's biggest arts festival
Artists and performers from around the globe
Children's parade
Free open-air events

i Information
♿ Generally excellent
£ Free - variable

cutting-edge performers

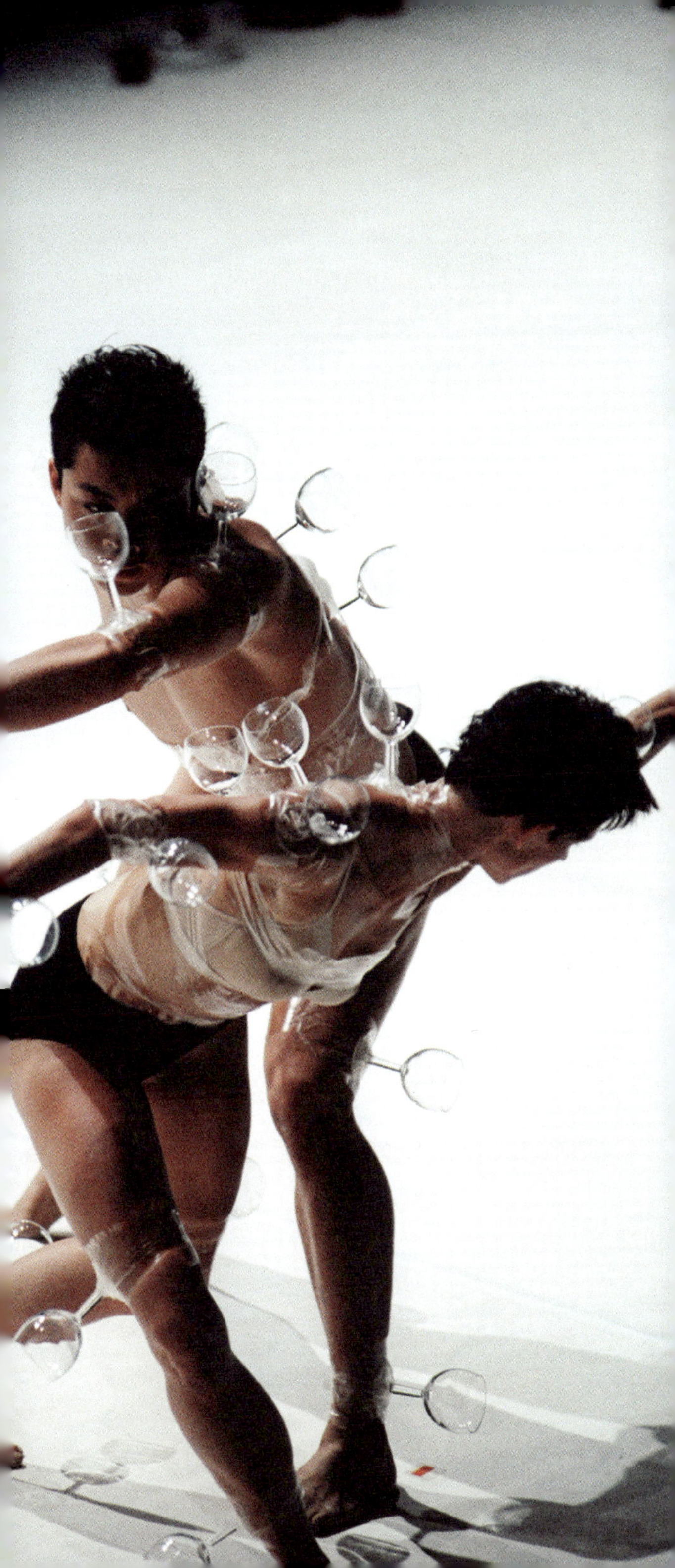

14
Brighton Marina

www.visitbrighton.com

Once dismissed as a misguided white elephant, in the past decade Brighton Marina has silenced doubters by enjoying an astonishing burst of growth. It is now the largest marina in Britain – boasting 1,500 berths, 800 homes, a multiplex cinema, casino and shopping complex, and numerous bars and restaurants.

i Brighton Marina Village
BN2 5UF

T (01273) 693636

www.brightonmarina.co.uk

※ Open all year round, 24 hours

Origins
Today's bustling marina owes its origins to the efforts of local entrepreneur Harry Cohen, who, in the early 60s, raised the possibility of Brighton gaining its own yacht harbour. With the backing of a consortium of banks and pension funds, he steered his proposals through two public enquiries, eventually gaining permission for the ambitious project through an Act of Parliament.

Opened by The Queen
Building started in 1971, with a 600-tonne crane having to be constructed in situ to haul into place the colossal concrete blocks needed for its foundations. It was to be six years before the first berths were installed, and a further one before the marina was officially opened by HM The Queen.

Award-winning Attraction
Located around a mile east of the city centre, the marina won the 2006 Best Place to Visit gong at the annual Brighton and Hove Business Awards. Its expansion continues, with a futuristic skyscraper and associated tower blocks, housing 853 new apartments – 40% of them 'affordable' – set to be added within the next two years.

★ Highlights
Largest marina in Britain

Factory retail outlet selling designer brands at 30% to 70% discounts

i Information
🍽 Cafés, bars, restaurants

♿ Good to excellent

£ Free

0906 711 2255*

15
Brighton Pier

Piers don't come much more grand, or garish, than Brighton's. Opened in 1899, the Palace Pier (or Brighton Pier, as it was renamed in 2000) is a non-stop pleasure zone crammed with amusement arcades, bingo halls, karaoke bars, candyfloss stalls and white-knuckle funfair rides.

- Madeira Drive BN2 1TW
- T (01273) 609361
- www.brightonpier.co.uk
- Open all year round 10-10

Vintage Charm
At first sight, the pier's attractions may seem a little old-fashioned and quaint for some tastes. But, for many families, it displays more than enough nostalgic charm to make an afternoon's stroll along its 1,722ft deck well worth the effort.

White-knuckle Rides
While the pier's funfair zone retains old-world mainstays like its ghost train and iconic helter skelter, these have now been joined by a rollercoaster and the recently installed Super Booster – a hair-raising experience which lifts four daring 'passengers' at a time 125ft into the air before plummeting them down at 60mph.

Film Location
Brighton Pier has been used as a location for several films, notably *Carry On at Your Convenience* and *Carry On Girls*, in which it was visited by the likes of Sid James and Joan Sims. In recognition of its continuing popularity – it currently attracts some three million visitors a year – the attraction won the National Pier Society's inaugural Pier of the Year title in 1998. It is open all year round, and entry is free.

★ Highlights
Thrilling fairground rides
Amusement arcades
Fortune-telling
Karaoke pub

i Information
🍴 Pubs, restaurants, food stalls
♿ Excellent
£ Free (rides vary)

*calls cost 50p per minute, UK only

16 Brighton Seafront

www.visitbrighton.com

Brighton's most popular attraction is its trademark pebble beach. Stretching more than six miles from its westernmost extremity, Hove Lagoon, to Rottingdean in the east, the sweeping seafront boasts uninterrupted vistas over the English Channel and is a year-round playground for swimmers, sailors, surfers and sun-seekers.

T (01273) 292716
www.visitbrighton.com

Fun for Everyone

The lower seafront walk between Brighton's two historic piers underwent major redevelopment in the 1990s, and has since become a flourishing area bristling with pastel-coloured artists' studios, souvenir shops, cafés and bars. A gentle stroll towards the West Pier ruins takes you past a succession of fishmongers, cockle stalls, public sculptures and fairground rides, as well as beach volleyball and basketball courts, sandpits and even a pitch reserved for a local French boules club.

Vibrant Nightlife

After dark, the seafront transforms into the city's most popular nocturnal haunt, its wide array of clubs offering an ever-changing programme of top DJs and specialist music nights. Genres catered for range from house, hip-hop and dance through funk to Indie and alternative rock.

Art in the Sand

Towards the marina lies Brighton's famous nudist beach. Beside this is a stretch of seafront that plays host to an annual sand-sculpture festival, with past exhibits including miniature versions of Egypt's Great Pyramid and Sphinx.

★ Highlights
Six miles of uninterrupted seafront
Public art
Sandpits, beach volleyball and boules pitches
Brighton Fishing Museum

i Information
🍽 Bars, cafés, restaurants, seafood stalls
♿ Excellent
£ Free

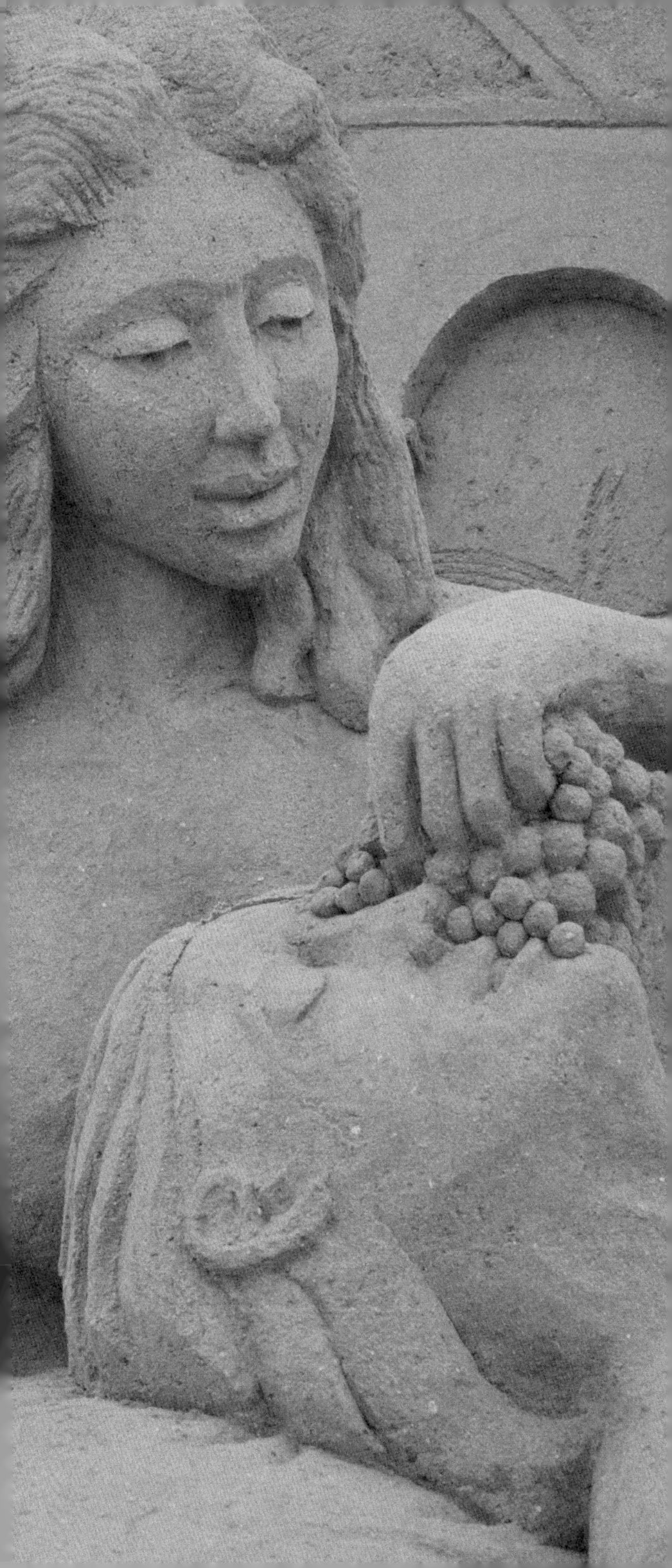

18
Burning the Clocks

www.visitbrighton.com

One of Brighton's most idiosyncratic and spectacular events is its annual Burning the Clocks festival – a vibrant street parade of giant paper and willow lanterns, mythical beasts and ghostly figures timed to coincide with the Winter Solstice. The free carnival culminates in an impressive bonfire and firework display on the beach to the east of the city.

i Through city centre, eastwards to Madeira Drive BN2

T (01273) 571106

www.burningtheclocks.co.uk

※ 21 December 6pm onwards

Peaceful Celebration
Now in its 13th year (2007), Burning the Clocks has become a Brighton institution, and is second only to the Lewes Bonfire celebrations in terms of sheer spectacle. Unlike the latter, though, which relive, in fiery glory, the religious tensions of the Jacobean era, the message of Burning the Clocks is a peaceful one.

Homemade Lanterns
The event's organisers, community arts group Same Sky, are keen to keep it a low-key affair – billing it as 'an antidote to the excesses of the commercial Christmas'. But that hasn't stopped them attracting an ever-growing number of participants and revellers – around 1,000 people regularly take part in lantern-making workshops, while the parade itself typically attracts 15,000 spectators.

Celebrity Backers
Burning the Clocks, organised in conjunction with local radio station *Juice FM*, also boasts an impressive list of sponsors, including locally based musician Fatboy Slim and the University of Brighton.

★ Highlights
Colourful, artistic homemade lantern parade
Spectacular seafront firework display and bonfire

i Information
♿ Good for parade, poor for fireworks
£ Free

the message is a peaceful one

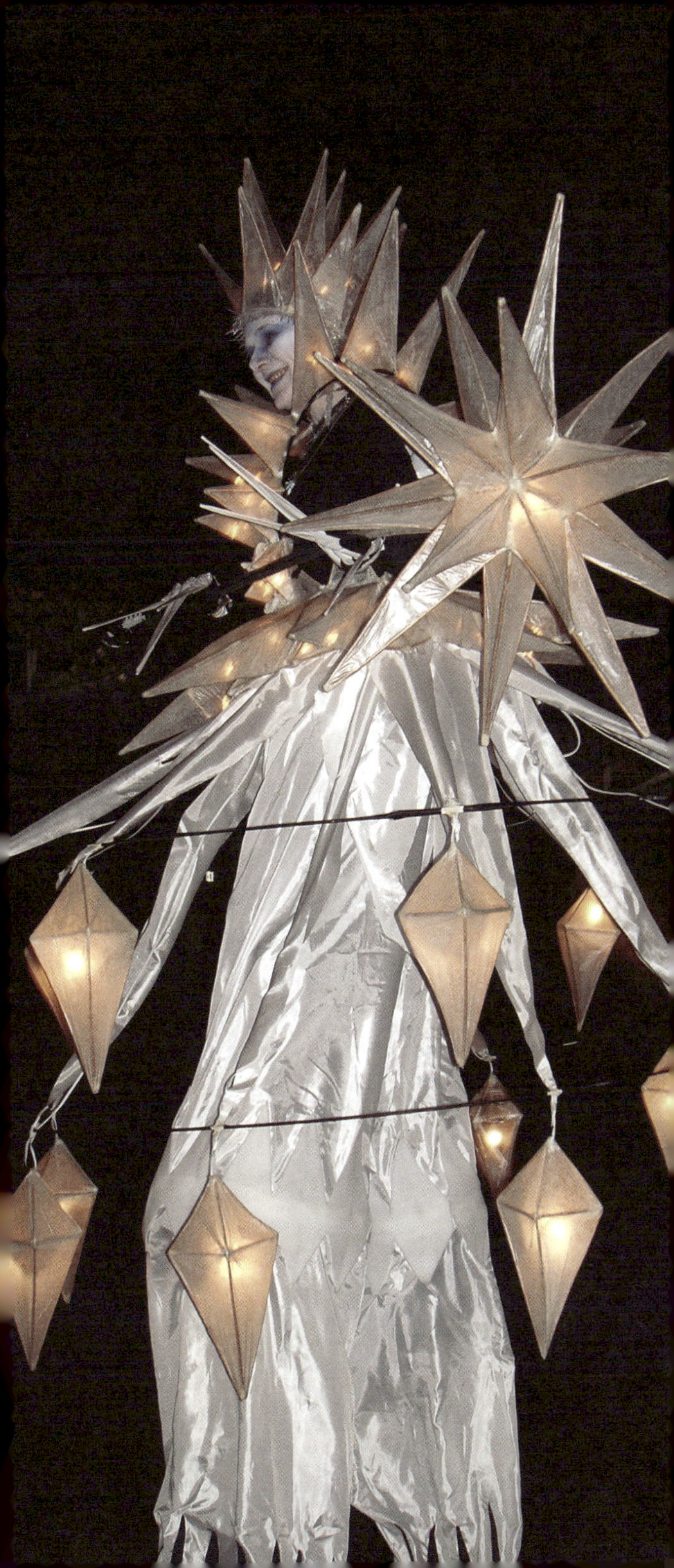

20 Charleston

www.visitbrighton.com

Set in an idyllic enclave a short drive off the A27 between the villages of Firle and Selmeston, this elegant early 18th century house was made famous as the rural retreat of the artists, writers and intellectuals known collectively as the Bloomsbury Group.

i Firle BN8 6LL
T (01323) 811265
www.charleston.org

April to Oct, Wed and Sat 11.30-6, Thurs, Fri, Sun, Bank Holiday 2-6. Last admission to house 5pm

Eccentric Decor
The house's handsome traditional facade belies an extraordinarily quirky interior – courtesy of its former owners, artists Vanessa Bell and Duncan Grant. On moving to Charleston in 1916, the couple began customising it to their bohemian tastes, painting the walls, doors and furniture in a style inspired by Italian frescoes and the Post-Impressionists. Charleston's walled garden was similarly re-designed, with mosaics, box hedges, ponds and classical statuary contributing to a new Mediterranean-style layout.

Bloomsbury
Bell once wrote of this period that it promised to 'be an odd life' – and it certainly wasn't run-of-the-mill.

Under the stewardship of Bell and Grant, Charleston became the favoured meeting-place of E M Forster, Lytton Strachey and Virginia and Leonard Woolf, whose own country home was in the nearby village of Rodmell.

Festival Time
Fittingly, Charleston now boasts its own literary festival, held each May. Among the highlights of last year's event were appearances by Booker Prize-winning author Peter Carey, historian Simon Schama and playwright Stephen Poliakoff.

★ Highlights
Stunning décor in Italian fresco and Post-Impressionist styles
Elegant early 18th-century architecture
Mediterranean-style formal garden
Annual literary festival

i Information
Café
Good to ground floor
£ House and garden
£6.50 adult; £6 concessions; £4.50 child 6-16; £17.50 family
£ Garden only
£2.50 adult; £1 child

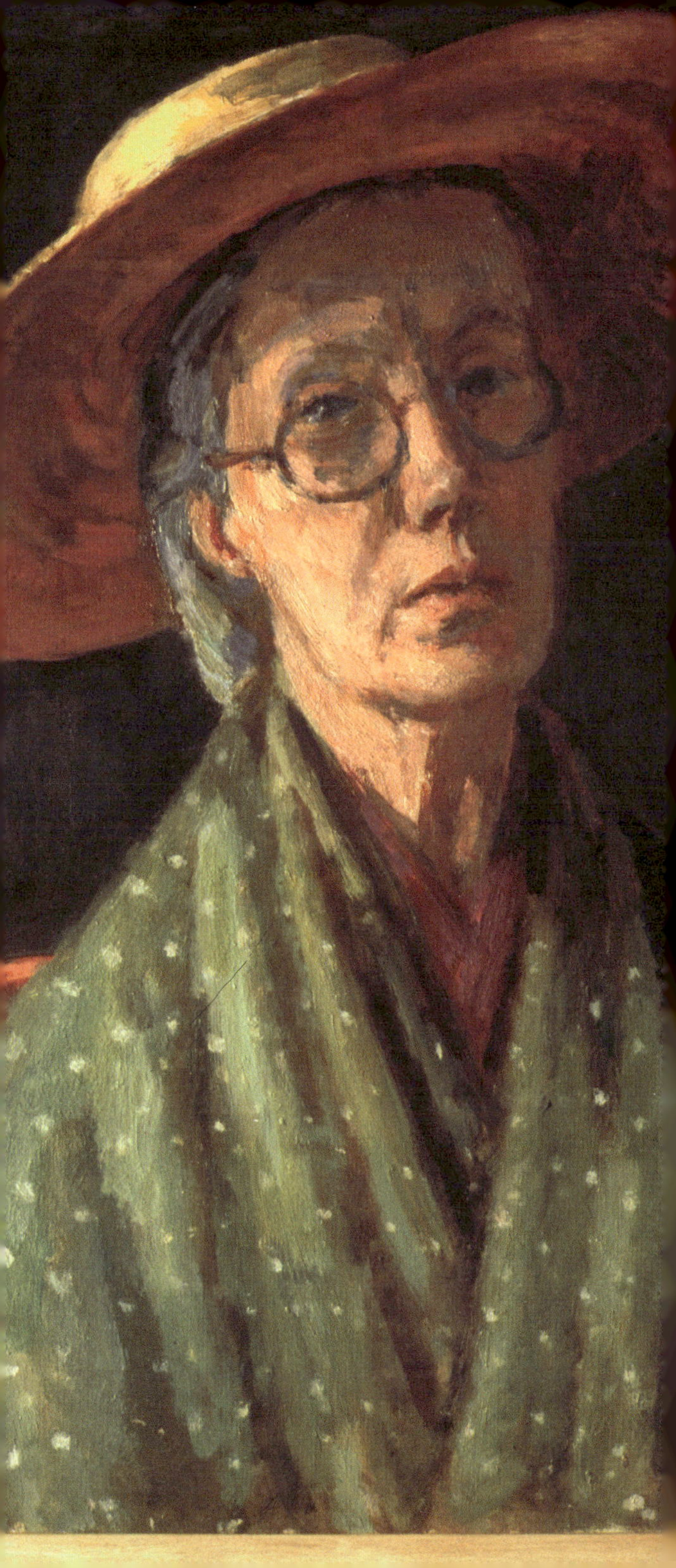

22
Devil's Dyke

www.visitbrighton.com

This impressive geological feature – the largest chalkland dry valley in England - is located 10 minutes' drive from Brighton and Hove. A favourite haunt among hang-gliders and hikers, it boasts unrivalled panoramic views over the Sussex coastline.

i Devil's Dyke BN6
T (01273) 857712
www.nationaltrust.org.uk

✸ All year round, 24 hours

The Devil's Work
Managed by the National Trust, legend has it the plunging valley was created by the Devil in an effort to flood the surrounding countryside. The extent of the damage caused by his nefarious deed could have been worse: he was reputedly interrupted when an old woman placed a lighted candle in her window.

Victorian Favourite
Whatever its true origins, the dyke remains one of Brighton's most famous landmarks, attracting scores of visitors each year. In Victorian times, it boasted two bandstands, an observatory, a *camera obscura* and, for the truly adventurous, an aerial cable railway. None of these survive today, but there is ample parking at its summit and an open-top bus service from Brighton Pier (vintage ones with conductors run on some Sundays).

Scenic Walks
A leisurely walk down the escarpment towards Fulking village will lead you into the rear garden of the family-friendly Shepherd and Dog pub. Be warned, though: if you've left your car up top or aim to catch the bus home, it's a steep climb back!

★ Highlights
Sweeping sea views
Largest chalkland dry valley in England

i Information
🍽 Pubs
♿ Good to limited
£ Free

one of Brighton's most famous landmarks

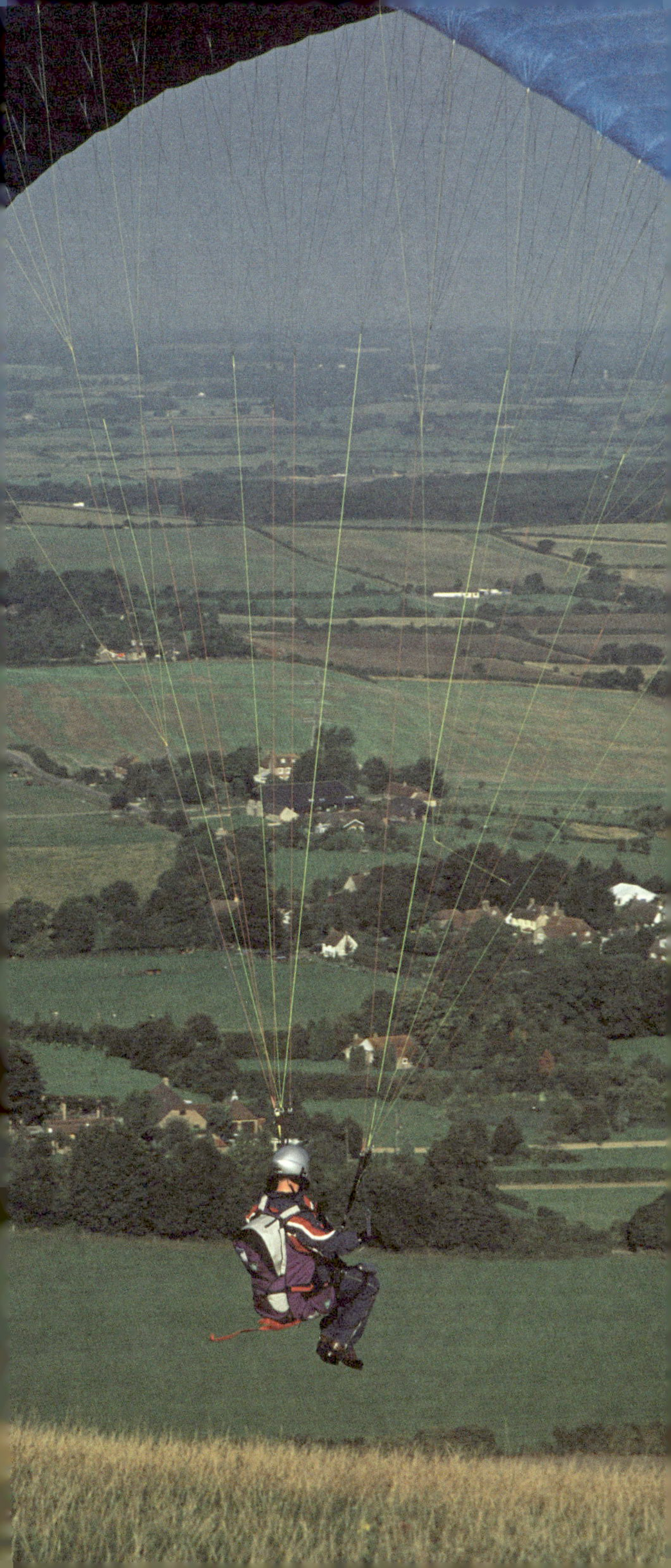

24 The Lanes

www.visitbrighton.com

Chock-full of fine restaurants, boutiques, gift shops and world-class jewellers, the picture-postcard Lanes is the highlight of many a Christmas shopping trip to Brighton.

i The Lanes BN1
T (0906) 711 2255
T (01273) 774000
www.brightonbusiness.co.uk/lbn

Open all year round. Individual shop opening times vary

Brighton's Oldest District

The oldest surviving area of the city centre, The Lanes was once the mercantile heart of Brighthelmstone. Burned down by French invaders in the 16th century, it was swiftly rebuilt, and today the narrow, cobbled alleys and tightly packed roofs at its centre are as close as modern Brighton gets to a living reminder of its Medieval past.

Alfresco Dining and People-Watching

Among the busiest spots in The Lanes is East Street, where tourists potter among craft stalls at weekends or sit sipping wine and dining alfresco while being entertained by traditional jazz or swing bands in the summer. Choices of eatery include The Sussex pub, English's seafood restaurant and various pizzerias.

Buzzing Centre

The area's focus is Brighton Square, where more than 20 shops and eateries cluster around a distinctive dolphin fountain built by sculptor James Osborne. Coins thrown into the water are donated to the city's Royal Alexandra Hospital for Sick Children.

As well as being Brighton's prime destination for quality souvenirs, The Lanes is also home to some of its most highly rated restaurants (see Eating and Drinking).

★ Highlights
Oldest district in Brighton and Hove
Narrow, historic shopping streets
Craft shops and designer boutiques

i Information
🍽 Cafés, pubs, restaurants
♿ Generally good but limited in parts
£ Free

0906 711 2255*

25

Lewes Bonfire Celebration

The internationally renowned Lewes Bonfire Celebration on 5 November isn't any ordinary Guy Fawkes' Night display. Opening with a series of overlapping torch-lit processions through the heart of the historic East Sussex county town, and lasting more than five hours, this mammoth carnival culminates in six simultaneous bonfires and firework shows at vantage points overlooking the centre.

i Lewes city centre and surrounds BN7

T (01273) 471516

www.lewesbonfirecouncil.org.uk

✹ 5 November, 6-11

Historical Legacy

Lewes's long love affair with Guy Fawkes' Night (a legacy of its staunchly Protestant past) dates back to 1853, when the town's first local bonfire societies, representing the central Lewes and Cliffe areas, were formed. Since then, they have been joined by four others – Commercial Square, South Street, Waterloo and Nevill Juvenile – each of which now operates its own route and bonfire site during the celebration.

Burning the Infamous

One of the event's highlights is a re-enactment of the burning of 17 Protestant martyrs in Lewes High Street between 1555 and 1557, under the reign of Mary Tudor. More controversial still is the burning of effigies not only of Guy Fawkes but of Pope Paul V (the pontiff at the time of the 1605 Gunpowder Plot), and various 'hate figures' of the day – including, in recent times, Saddam Hussein and Osama bin Laden.

★ Highlights

Six spectacular fancy dress parades and bonfires

Burning effigies of notorious historical and contemporary figures

Firework displays

i Information

🍽 Cafés, pubs, restaurants, food stalls

♿ Good to limited

£ Free

*calls cost 50p per minute, UK only

26
Lewes Castle

www.visitbrighton.com

This sturdy Medieval stronghold occupies a central position overlooking Lewes. One of only two double-motted castles known in England, it was begun shortly after the Norman Conquest, by William the Conqueror's chief justiciar, William de Warenne, and finally completed 300 years later with the addition of its impressive barbican gate.

i High Street, Lewes BN7 1YE
T (01273) 486290
www.sussexpast.co.uk

Tues-Sat 10-5.30. Sun, Mon & Bank Hols 11-5.30.
Closed Mondays in Jan and 24-26 December.
Castle closes at dusk in winter

Occupied through the Ages

Though its heyday was in the Middle Ages, Lewes Castle retained significant historical connections throughout its centuries-long occupation. One of its later owners was Thomas Read Kemp, a 19th-century MP for Lewes and founder of Kemp Town, the Brighton village renowned for its magnificent Georgian architecture.

Museum

Today, Lewes Castle is one of the most popular tourist attractions in the historic market town. Before clambering to the summit of its bailey, why not visit the Barbican House Museum beneath it to read up on its history? Maintained by the Sussex Archaeological Society, the museum houses an extensive collection of local artefacts, a changing temporary exhibition gallery, and a specialist bookshop.

Cut-price Tickets

Joint tickets for the castle and Anne of Cleves House can also be purchased, and there are discounts for children and OAPs.

★ Highlights
One of only two double-motted castles in England
Panoramic views over Lewes and surrounding countryside
Archaeological museum

i Information
♿ Good to museum, limited to castle
£ £4.70 adult, (£4.20 OAP/student), £2.40 child, £12.20 family (two adults, two children), £9.50 family (one adult, four children), £2.40 disabled and carer

0906 711 2255*

27
London to Brighton Mini Run

Now in its 22nd year (2007), this annual rally sees central Brighton transformed into a scene reminiscent of classic Michael Caine movie The Italian Job, as a convoy of multicoloured Minis pours down to the seafront to rapturous applause from onlookers.

i Finish at Madeira Drive BN2

enquiries@london-to-brighton.co.uk
www.london-to-brighton.co.uk

❋ Third Sunday in May, 8.30-5

Popularity
The popular spectator event, organised by the London and Surrey Mini Owners' Club, normally takes place on the third Sunday in May, and is now so over-subscribed by would-be drivers hoping to take part in recent times that the number of tickets has been rationed to 2,100 with priority given to club members.

Driving Down South
Commencing at Crystal Palace Park, Penge (where many entrants camp the night before), the 60–mile run finishes at Madeira Drive, opposite Brighton Pier. Once here, weary participants traditionally pull over for a well-earned glass of champagne or beer at one of the many nearby bars, while watching crowds gather to admire their colourfully decorated vehicles.

Charity Sponsorship
As with the London Marathon and other major rallies, including the London to Brighton Bike Ride, there is an important charity element to the Mini run, with many drivers raising sponsorship money for good causes. The organisers also host their own fundraising auction, nominating a different beneficiary each year.

★ Highlights
Colourful rally of modern and vintage minis

i Information
♿ Excellent
£ Free to spectators

*calls cost 50p per minute, UK only

28 London to Brighton Veteran Car Run

www.visitbrighton.com

With their tooting horns, chugging engines and brightly painted bonnets, the vintage vehicles entered for this century-old Brighton-bound rally provide a welcome splash of colour as the winter evenings draw in.

i Finish at Madeira Drive BN2
www.vccofgb.co.uk

❀ First Sunday in November 7-5

1896 Vintage
The inaugural 'Emancipation Run' (as it was originally called) was held on 14 November 1896, to celebrate the passage of the Locomotives on the Highway Act. This landmark law abolished the speed limit for 'light locomotives' (cars) from four to 14mph, as well as the requirement for them to be preceded by men waving red flags. The initial run wasn't an unqualified success: of the 33 cars to attempt the 60 miles from London's Metropole Hotel to its namesake on Brighton's Kings Road, only 14 completed the journey.

Annual Event
This stuttering start failed to stop the event becoming an annual fixture, and it is now the longest-running motoring event in the world. Among the most famous cars to have taken part is a vintage Daimler originally owned by King Edward VII and entered (though not driven) by HM The Queen in 1971. Her cousin, Prince Michael of Kent, president of the Royal Automobile Club, regularly participates.

Oldies Only
Eligibility is subject to several strict criteria – not the least being the requirement that your car was manufactured before 1 January 1905.

★ Highlights
Longest-running amateur car rally in the world
Hundreds of colourful vintage motor vehicles

i Information
♿ Excellent
£ Free to spectators

longest-running motoring event in the world

don to Brighton Veteran Car

Finish

AW 38

V.C.C.
1902
JAMES
AND
BROWNE

173

30 North Laine

www.visitbrighton.com

Famed for its colourful shop-fronts, cosmopolitan cafés and funky, bohemian atmosphere, North Laine is one of the jewels in the crown of Brighton city centre. With more than 300 shops, 22 pubs, four theatres and two museums to its name, it is equally popular among culture vultures and shopaholics.

- North Laine BN1
- T (01273) 601641
- www.northlaine.co.uk
- Open all year round. Individual shop opening times vary

Bohemian Rhapsody

North Laine first began flourishing in the 1830s, in the wake of the Prince Regent's adoption of Brighton as his home from home. Nearly two centuries on, it boasts the most eclectic array of small, independently owned retailers on the South Coast – from traditional craft shops through flea markets, second-hand bookshops and retro clothing stores to fiercely modern designer boutiques.

Retro Chic

On a sunny afternoon, strolling along Gardner Street or Kensington Gardens can feel like stepping back in time to the Sixties, as you pass lean-to stalls festooned with exotic fabrics, original artwork, vintage jackets and jewellery. As bargain-hunters peruse the cluttered shelves of bric-a-brac in Snoopers' Paradise, vinyl collectors would do well to spend time browsing through the racks of the numerous record shops.

Upwardly Mobile

North Laine has recently become a magnet for affluent professionals seeking to move out of London – a trend reflected in its various new luxury residential developments.

★ Highlights

- Widest selection of independent shops in South
- Colourful, bohemian café and bar culture
- Haven for record and book collectors

i Information

- Pubs, cafés, restaurants
- Generally good
- £ Free

BRIGHTON

NORTH LAINE

ROYAL PAVILION

THEA...

THE LA...

SEAFR...

MUS...

LIBR...

32 Preston Manor

www.visitbrighton.com

Winter closure – closed to the general public from 1 October to 31 March

- Preston Drove BN1 6SD
- T (01273) 292770
- www.prestonmanor.virtualmuseum.info/
- April-Sept Tues-Sat 10-5, Sun 2-5. Closed Mon

Architectural Mix
This 'haunted' mansion on the edge of Preston Park is a curious architectural hybrid. Originally constructed in around 1600, it was rebuilt in 1738 and substantially enlarged in 1905 – a year to which it owes many of its most enduring features.

Class Act
In many ways the epitome of the 'upstairs, downstairs' Edwardian manor, Preston Manor offers a revealing insight into the lives of the early 20th-century gentry. Set over four storeys, it offers public access to some 20 rooms, ranging from the butler's pantry and kitchens in its basement to the plush bedrooms and nursery on its top floor.

Ghoulies and Ghosties
One of the manor's biggest draws, however, remains its periodic ghost tours, frequently held during the autumn and winter months, when it is otherwise closed to visitors. Among the grizzly manifestations reputedly witnessed at the house have been a disembodied hand floating beside a four-poster bed; a body buried under a patio; and the spirit of a mysterious 'White Lady', which allegedly appeared during the filming of a recent episode of the LIVINGtv ghost detective series, *Most Haunted*.

The manor's grounds incorporate a splendid walled garden, the 13th-century parish church of St Peter, and a lovingly tended pet cemetery.

★ Highlights
Four storeys of antique décor dating from 17th to 20th centuries

Beautiful walled garden

Information
- Good to ground floor
- £ £4 adult (£3.30 concessions), £2.30 child under 16, £10.30 family (two adults, four children), £6.30 family (one adult, two children)

Photographs: © The Royal Pavilion, Libraries & Museums, Brighton & Hove

34
Royal Pavilion

www.visitbrighton.com

With its Taj Mahal-like exterior and sumptuous banqueting room, the Royal Pavilion is Brighton's most spectacular and oft-photographed landmark. Set in beautiful gardens and open throughout the year, this gaudy but glorious architectural conceit, designed for the Prince Regent, was modelled on an idealised Indian 'pleasure palace'.

i Pavilion Buildings BN1 1EE
T (01273) 290900
www.royalpavilion.org.uk

Oct to March: 10-5.15 (last tickets 4.30pm), April to Sept: 9.30-5.45 (last tickets 5pm). Closed from 2.30pm on 24 Dec and all day 25 and 26 Dec

Full of Eastern Promise
Begun in 1787 by Henry Holland, the Marine Pavilion, as it was originally known, started life as a neo-Classical conversion of a former farmhouse. Between 1815 and 1823, it underwent a startling transformation under the hand of John Nash, who, at the behest of the Prince (by then King George IV), superimposed an intricate cast iron framework over the façade of the existing building, incorporating its trademark 'onion' domes and minarets.

Regency Decadence
Though it is for its incongruous exterior (lovingly refurbished in the 1980s) that the pavilion is best known, the building's internal décor is equally extravagant. The music room, the work of the King's personal designer, Frederick Crace, boasts a domed ceiling covered in a mosaic of gilded scallop shells, while elsewhere walls and furniture are adorned with serpentine dragons and golden palm trees.

Getting Married
As well as being one of Brighton's most popular attractions, today the pavilion is also licensed for civil weddings.

★ Highlights
Taj Mahal-style exterior façade
Sumptuous Indian-influenced interior
Queen Victoria's bedroom
Beautiful gardens

i Information
🍽 Café
♿ Excellent on ground floor
£ £7.50 adult (£5.75 concessions), £5 child under 16, £19 family (two adults, two children), £11.50 family (one adult, two children)

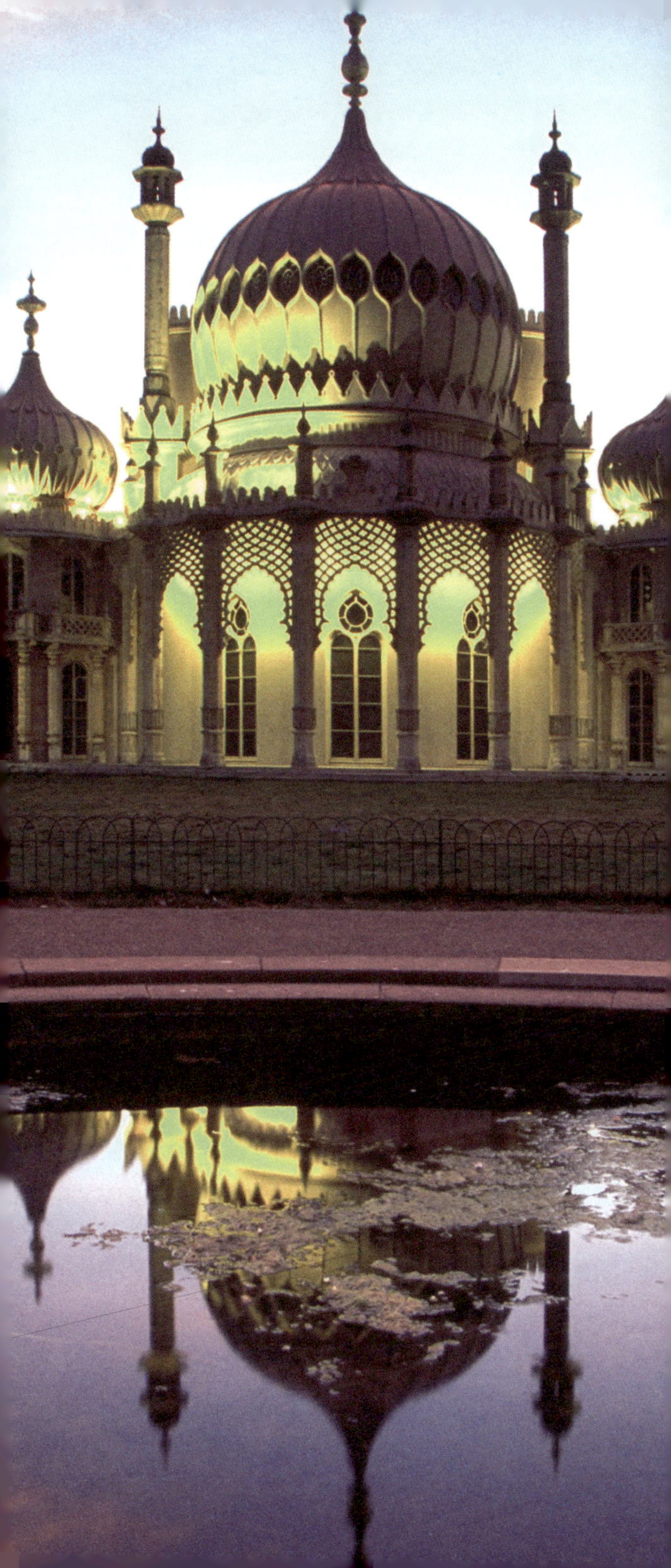

36
Sea Life Centre

www.visitbrighton.com

Housed in an imposing Victorian building flanked by a pillared forecourt, Brighton's Sea Life Centre is the oldest operating aquarium in the world. The immensely popular family-friendly attraction contains more than 30 marine and freshwater habitats, and is home to some 150 species – including sharks, giant spider crabs and piranhas.

- Madeira Drive BN2 1TB
- (01273) 604234
- www.sealifeeurope.com
- Daily 10-6. Last admission 5pm. Ring for winter times.

Clock Tower
Designed by Eugenius Birch, the original aquarium was an eccentric amalgam of gothic and Italianate styles, incorporating grand archways and columns. The decision to set its foundations deep in the ground (a facet emphasised by the steep steps leading down into it) was the result of a diktat by the local authorities that it must not be taller than the neighbouring promenade, Marine Parade. This stipulation was ignored with the addition, in 1874, of a clock tower decorated with bronze statues symbolising the four seasons.

Performing Dolphins
Rebuilt in a neoclassical style in the 1920s, the aquarium subsequently became a dolphinarium, but a growing backlash against the use of performing animals saw this closed in 1991. Now a Sea Life Centre, it has a reputation for ecological awareness.

Marine Monsters
Among its latest additions is Venom, an area in which visitors are invited to stand inches from poison arrow frogs, lion fish and sea snakes.

★ Highlights
More than 150 sea species housed in 30 habitats
Impressive Victorian design by architect of West Pier
New Venom exhibition of poisonous sea life

i Information	
🍽	Café
♿	Good
£	£10.95 adult (£8.50 OAP/student), £7.95 child three to 14, £34.90 family

37 Volk's Railway

0906 711 2255*

One of the mainstays of 'old' Brighton, this endearing seafront attraction was the first public electric railway in the world. Built from scratch by the pioneering Victorian inventor Magnus Volk, it opened for business for the first time on 4 August 1883.

- Madeira Drive BN2 1EN
- T (01273) 292718
- www.brighton-hove.gov.uk
- April to Sept: Mon-Fri 11-5, Sat and Sun 11-6

Getting Your Sea Legs

Originally stretching for a mere quarter of a mile, between the aquarium and Brighton's long-since demolished Chain Pier, the railway took passengers far further out to sea than its modern-day equivalent – veering 50 to 100 yards offshore, precariously balanced on stilts. As a result of the somewhat absurd appearance of this section of track, the railway swiftly earned the nickname 'Daddy-Longlegs'.

Trains to the Marina

Some 120 years later, the railway extends more than a mile along the seafront to the east of Brighton Pier. Modern health and safety concerns ensure it follows a rather less hazardous route than in former times, taking a straight course between stations at the aquarium and Black Rock, on the western edge of Brighton Marina.

Low-price Fares

The popular, family-friendly attraction remains excellent value for money with special deals for children and OAPs. It also has full disabled access and can carry up to 40 passengers at a time.

★ Highlights
- First public electric railway in the world
- Daily trips in spring and summer from Brighton Pier to marina
- Sweeping sea views

i Information
- ♿ Excellent
- £ £2.50 adult return (£1.70 OAP), £1.20 child, £6 family

*calls cost 50p per minute, UK only

endearing seafront attraction

38
West Pier Ruins

www.visitbrighton.com

Long earmarked for reconstruction, the derelict West Pier is now a rusting skeleton thanks to protracted planning disputes and a succession of violent storms. But the dramatic silhouette of Britain's only Grade I listed pier remains one of Brighton and Hove's most iconic landmarks.

- Kings Road BN1 2FL
- (01273) 321499
- www.westpier.co.uk
- All year round, 24 hours

Iconic Grandeur
Designed by Eugenius Birch, it started life in 1866, when cast iron columns were screwed into the seabed and a makeshift promenade deck installed. Initially it was a modest affair, boasting only four Oriental-style 'houses', and glass screens at its end to protect visitors from the elements. Between 1875 and 1916, it became grander, gaining first a bandstand, then steamer landing stages, and finally a concert hall.

Weathering the Storms
The pier closed in 1975 due to storm damage. Since then, a series of consortia – including one fronted by former world champion boxer Chris Eubank – have pledged to restore it to its former glory. While the dream of a wholesale rebuild was abandoned following the recent withdrawal of a long-earmarked £19 million Heritage Lottery Fund grant, plans are still afoot for a privately funded partial reconstruction.

Future Plans
David Marks and Julia Barfield, award-winning designers of the London Eye, recently announced plans to build Brighton i-360 – a towering observation mast with an aero-dynamically designed pod capable of lifting 100 passengers 490ft into the air – on the West Pier site.

★ Highlights
Iconic ruins of Britain's only Grade I listed pier

Peace Statue

i Information
- Excellent views
- £ Free

Credit: ianpack.co.uk

Computer generated image of Brighton i360

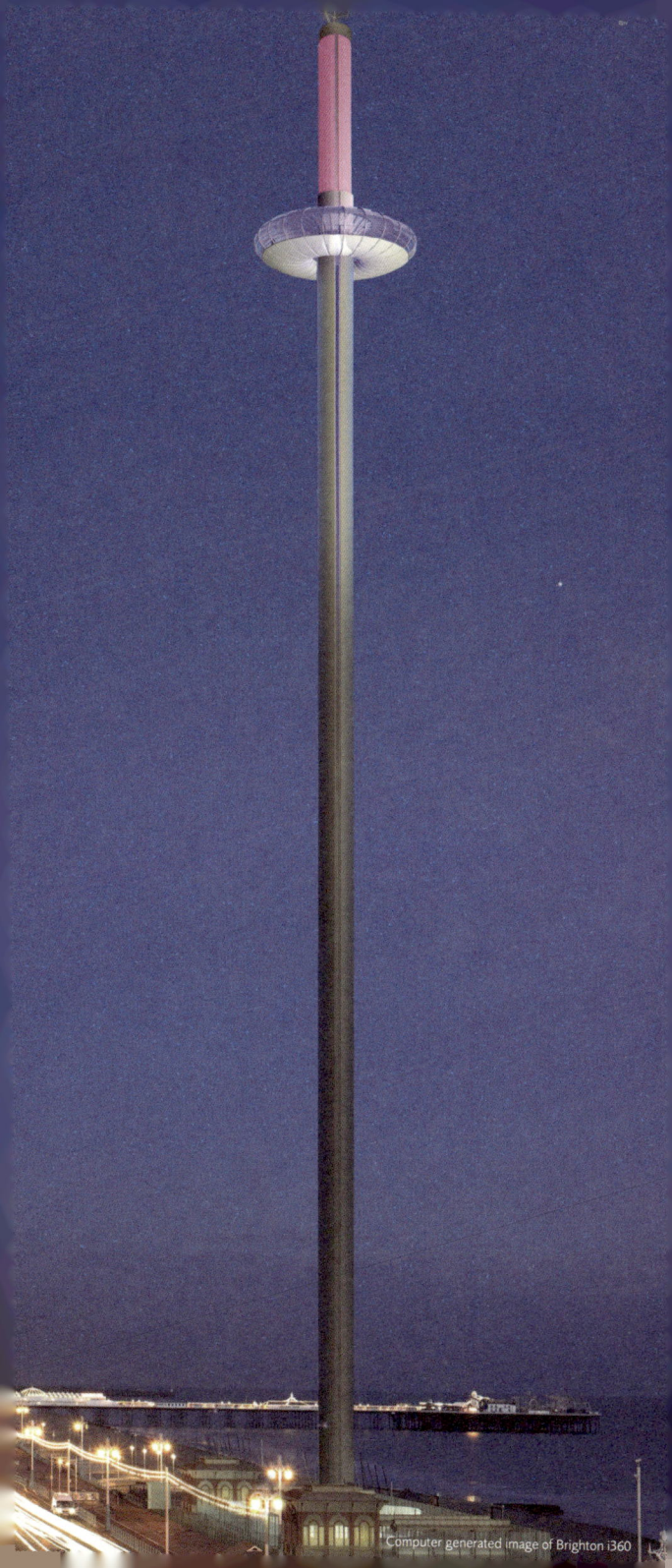

40 Other Major Attractions

The Bluebell Railway
This beautifully restored stretch of steam railway, near Haywards Heath, was reopened in 1960. Run by volunteers, it is one of the foremost attractions in Sussex.

- *i* Sheffield Park Station TN22 3QL
- **T** (01825) 720825
  www.bluebell-railway.co.uk
- 1 April to 29 Oct (trains run daily)
- Variable (call 01825 720800 to book)
- **£** All line tickets from £4.50. One stop tickets from £4.40. Child, family and senior fares available. Special events available.

Brighton Racecourse
Immortalised in Graham Greene's Brighton Rock, this long-established attraction still draws huge crowds, thanks to its increasingly varied fixtures and hospitality packages.

- *i* Freshfield Road BN2 9XZ
- **T** (01273) 603 580
  www.brighton-racecourse.co.uk
- Phone for details of race meetings
- Bars, restaurant, food stalls
- Good
- **£** £30 Raceday package. £20 Fancy a flutter package. Phone for prices of individual race meetings.

Drusillas Zoo Park
Located near Alfriston, a 12-mile drive from Brighton, this popular and child-friendly zoo boasts penguins, monkeys, wild cats and numerous rides, including a safari train.

- *i* Alfriston BN26 5QS
- **T** (01323) 874100
  www.drusillas.co.uk
- Daily 10-5 (summer), 10-4 (winter). Closed Christmas Day
- Café, restaurant
- Excellent
- **£ Peak:** £12.25 adult, £11.25 child and OAP, £10.25 disabled and carer, £22.50-£56.25 family (depending on size)
  Standard: £11.50 adult, £10.50 child and OAP, £9.50 disabled and carer, £21-£52.50 family (depending on size)
  Off-peak: £10 adult, £9 child and OAP, £8 disabled and carer, £18-£45 family (depending on size)

The Long Man of Wilmington
This 235ft tall chalk giant – Europe's largest human representation – has mystified archaeologists for generations. Located near Firle, 30 minutes' drive from Brighton.

- *i* Windover Hill, Wilmington BN8
- **T** (01273) 487188
  www.sussexpast.co.uk
- All year long, 24 hours
- Poor
- **£** Free

Europe's largest human representation

Other Major Attractions

0906 711 2255*

41

Michelham Priory

Dating back to 1229, this Augustinian priory boasts England's longest Medieval water-filled moat. Attractions include a working watermill and annual sculpture trail.

- *i* Upper Dicker BN27 3QS
- **T** (01323) 849141

    www.sussexpast.co.uk

- ❋ March to October, Tue to Sun 10.30-4.30, except April-July and Sept (10.30-5) and Aug (10.30-5.30)
- 🍽 Picnic area
- ♿ Good

£6 adult (£5 OAP/student), £3 child under 15, £15 family (two adults, two children), £3 disabled and carer

Middle Farm

This 625-acre working farm is located at the foot of Firle Beacon, six miles east of Lewes. Boasts an organic food shop – and the largest collection of ciders in the world.

- *i* Firle BN8 6LJ
- **T** (01323) 811411

    www.middlefarm.com

- ❋ Daily 10-7
- 🍽 Restaurant
- ♿ Excellent
- **£** £2.50 adult or child
    Free child under three

The Regency Town House

Based in Brunswick Square, this Grade I listed 1820s house is being developed into a heritage centre focusing on the city's architecture between the 1780s and 1840s.

- *i* Brunswick Square BN3 1EH
- **T** (01273) 206306

    www.rth.org.uk

- ❋ Early spring to late autumn (guided tours only)
- ♿ Limited
- **£** £5 adult or child

West Blatchington Windmill

Split over five floors, this restored Grade II listed windmill dating from the 1820s still contains its original workings. Exhibits include an antique thresher and oat-crusher.

- *i* Holmes Avenue BN3 7LE
- **T** (01273) 776017

    www.blatchington.
    virtualmuseum.info

- ❋ May to Sept, Sun and Bank Hol 2.30-5
- 🍽 Café
- ♿ Good to ground floor
- **£** £1 adult, 50p child

---

*calls cost 50p per minute, UK only

heritage centre focusing on architecture

42 Architecture, Heritage and Galleries

Brighton Museum and Art Gallery

- Royal Pavilion Gardens BN1 1EE
- T (01273) 290900
- www.brighton.virtualmuseum.info/
- Tuesday 10-7, Wed-Sat 10-5, Sun 2-5. Closed Mon, except public holidays (10-5). Closed 24-27 December

Following a £10 million redevelopment, Brighton Museum and Art Gallery recently reopened to rave reviews. Boasting imaginative new galleries, an elegant balcony café (see Eating and Drinking, p58) and free entry to all exhibitions, this once tired-looking museum has reinvigorated itself to become one of the city's premier tourist attractions.

First opened in 1873, the museum quickly established itself as a showcase for the fashions of the era. Capitalising on Brighton's growing popularity as a holiday destination for princes, it began by specialising in clothing design, furniture and the decorative arts. By the mid-20th century it housed some of the most impressive collections outside London, with notable highlights including its extensive ranges of Art Nouveau, Art Deco and Surrealist artefacts – including Mae West's Lips, a bizarre mouth-shaped sofa designed by Salvador Dali.

Today, the museum is entered from the neighbouring Pavilion Gardens. Its ambitious redesign, incorporating a large glass-fronted shop and a lift to allow wheelchair access to the first floor, was short-listed in 2003 for the £100,000 Gulbenkian Prize for Museums and Galleries. Recent high-profile visiting exhibitions have focused on the work of Rex Whistler, wartime painter and one of the Bright Young Things, and Paula Rego.

★ Highlights

Huge collection of Art Nouveau, Art Deco and Surrealist treasures

Free visiting exhibitions of work by major artists

Shortlisted for 2003 Gulbenkian Prize for Museums and Galleries

i Information

- Café
- Excellent
- £ Free/inexpensive

Art Nouveau, Art Deco and Surrealist

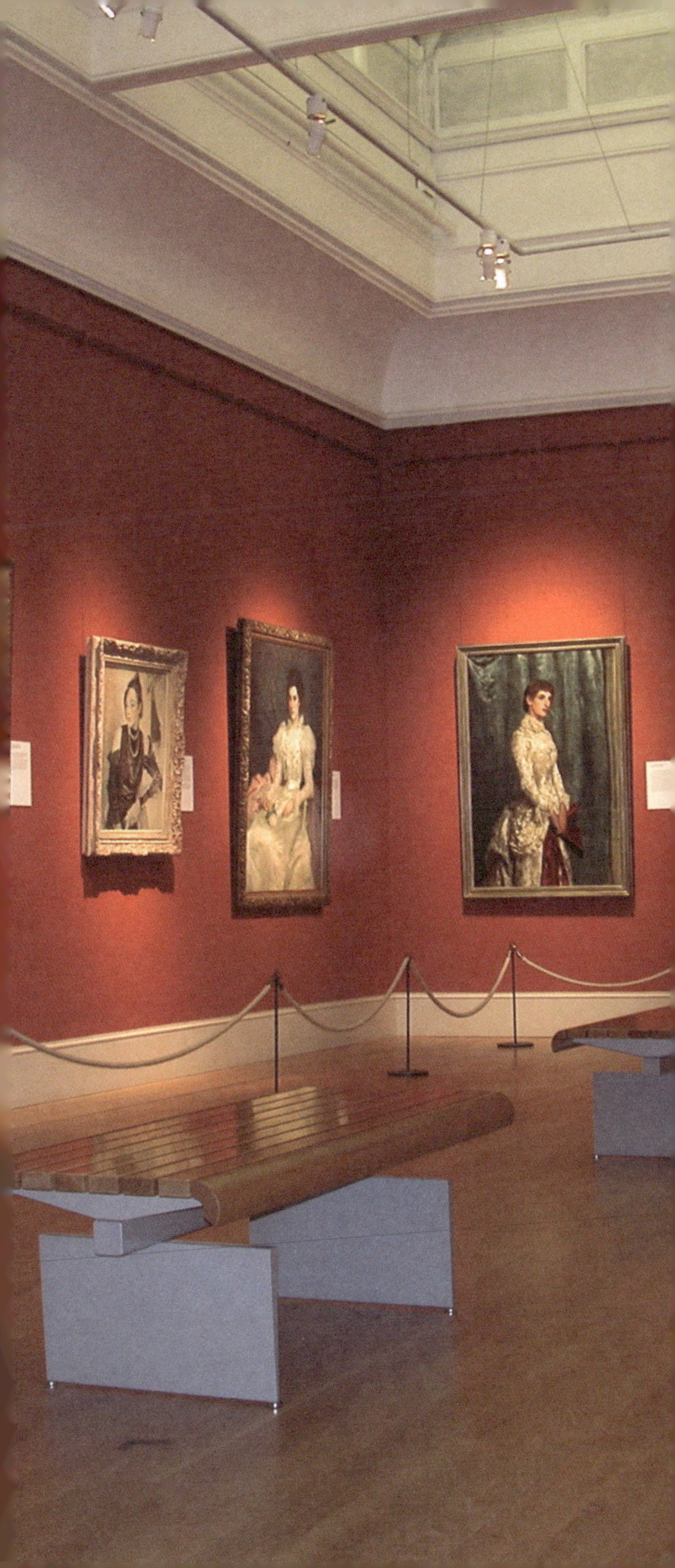

44 Architecture, Heritage and Galleries

www.visitbrighton.com

Embassy Court

i Kings Road BN1 2PX
friends@embassycourt.org
www.embassycourt.org

✽ Open for guided tours only on request

Built between 1934 and 1936, this Grade II* listed seafront apartment block resembles a hybrid of Oriental pagoda and luxury ocean liner. Following the first phase of an ongoing multi-million pound restoration, it has regained its rightful reputation as one of the most glorious examples of Art Deco architecture in Britain.

Embassy Court was the crowning glory of Wells Coates, a leading proponent of the Modernist Movement. Inspired by his travels in Japan, he resolved to replicate the clean lines and sultry curves then gaining popularity there in Brighton.

In its heyday, Embassy Court must have seemed like the lap of futurist luxury to its wealthy residents – who, at one time or other, included Graham Greene, Lord Olivier, Sir Rex Harrison and Diana Dors. In addition to its sun-trap balconies and sweeping sea views, it boasted a basement restaurant and concierge service.

Like many of the city's larger residential buildings, Embassy Court passed through a succession of landlords in the 1980s and 90s. But after years of neglect, its freehold was seized by the Crown in 1997, paving the way for refurbishment under the auspices of a company formed by some of its leaseholders, Bluestorm Ltd, and the designer, Sir Terence Conran.

★ Highlights
Pioneering Grade II* listed Modernist building
Guided tours

i Information
♿ Good
£ moderate

lap of futuristic luxury

Credit: ianpack.co.uk
Credit: ianpack.co.uk

0906 711 2255*

Architecture, Heritage and Galleries 45

Fabrica

- Holy Trinity Church, Duke Street BN1 1AG
- **T** (01273) 778646
- www.fabrica.org.uk

- Mon and Wed to Sat 11.30-5, Sun 2-5

Housed in the converted Holy Trinity Church on the outskirts of The Lanes, this innovative, artist-led gallery aims to foster greater public understanding of contemporary art and craft.

Fabrica was set up in 1996, with the help of grants from South East Arts, Brighton and Hove Council and The Foundation for Sport and the Arts. Since its small beginnings, it has built up a reputation for staging highly conceptual, but unpretentious and accessible, exhibitions. Among those who have exhibited there is the disabled artist Alison Lapper, whose 1999 photographic show featuring photographs of her naked and cradling her baby son, Parys, famously challenged conventional ideas about physical normality and beauty.

Fabrica, which has a free admissions policy, is currently in the midst of a five-year programme of events designed to promote specific aspects of contemporary art. Its annual schedule rotates on a seasonal basis with spring focusing on crafts; summer on materials-based installations; autumn on photography; and winter on digital arts.

As well as its exhibition space, the venue houses a free drop-in advisory service for professional artists who share its aspirations, designed to help them develop their skills. It can also be hired for conferences and other events.

★ Highlights
- Impressive ecclesiastical architecture
- Regular free exhibitions by cutting-edge artists
- Free drop-in advice service for local artists

i Information
- **&** Excellent
- **£** free/inexpensive

*calls cost 50p per minute, UK only

46 Architecture, Heritage and Galleries

www.visitbrighton.com

Hove Museum and Art Gallery

- New Church Road BN3 4AB
- (01273) 290200
- www.hove.virtualmuseum.info/
- Tues to Sat 10-5, Sun 2-5

Located on a tree-lined residential street in deepest Hove, this compact and charming museum, housed in a splendid Italianate Victorian villa, has recently undergone a £900,000 redevelopment.

Hove Museum and Art Gallery opened to the public in 1927, after the Brighton Corporation acquired Brooker Hall from its then owner for £4,000. The house had been built for John Oliver Vallance, based on a design by architect Thomas Lainson. It had been used, variously, as a residence by the Vallance family; a holding house for prisoners of war between 1914 and 1918; and a block of flats.

Today, the museum is a model of ergonomic design, with two of its permanent features, the Barnes Collection, charting Brighton and Hove's role in the birth of cinema, and the National Toy Museum and Institute of Play Collection, wrapped snugly into a double-sided exhibition space on its first floor. A wheelchair and buggy-friendly lift, decorated inside with colourful relief images of Heath Robinson-style contraptions, is tucked neatly into a tight, but manageable, corridor on the ground floor.

After spending a pleasant hour or two browsing through the displays, you'll be pleased to discover refreshment is available in an elegant Edwardian-style tearoom, Specialities include mouth-watering giant cream meringues and scones.

★ Highlights
- Graceful Italianate architecture
- Charts Brighton and Hove's role in birth of cinema
- National Toy Museum and Institute of Play Collection

i Information
- Tearoom
- Excellent
- £ free/inexpensive

the birth of cinema

0906 711 2255*

Architecture, Heritage and Galleries

47

Jubilee Library

i Jubilee Street BN1 1GE
T (01273) 290800
www.citylibraries.info/libraries/jubilee.asp

🌸 Mon and Tue 10-7,
Wed and Fri 10-5,
Thurs 10-8, Sat 10-4

Barely two years old, Brighton's futuristic new £14 million central library has won numerous prizes for its innovative, eco-friendly design – including the prestigious 2005 Prime Minister's Better Public Building Award and the title of Best Public Building in the South East from the Royal Institute of British Architects (RIBA).

Located a short walk from the Komedia theatre, Brighton Museum and Art Gallery and the Royal Pavilion, the library is at the heart of a new 'cultural quarter', which will soon include a One boutique hotel and a continental-style piazza.

Key to its uniqueness is its light, airy atmosphere and efficient use of energy. Designed to exploit the temperate local climate, it draws the sun's rays through its massive glass front wall and uses them to generate insulation by slowly releasing the heat gathered into its interior. It even uses recycled rainwater to flush its toilets.

The old Brighton Library, based in the Corn Exchange building, was often criticised for its limited collection, but this issue has been addressed with the opening of the new site. Jubilee Library houses 140,000 books, journals, paintings, DVDs, videos, audio-books and toys, and hosts regular free community events, as well as literary nights throughout the Brighton Festival.

★ Highlights
Multi award-winning 'eco library' with solar-fuelled heating
More than 140,000 items in collection

i Information
♿ Excellent
£ free/inexpensive

*calls cost 50p per minute, UK only

innovative, eco-friendly design

Credit: ianpack.co.uk

Credit: ianpack.co.uk

48 Architecture, Heritage and Galleries

Other Attractions

The Artists' Quarter
- Kings Road Arches BN1 1NB
  www.brighton-hove.gov.uk
- All year round, opening times vary

Collection of colourful and eclectic art and craft galleries located beneath the promenade on Brighton beachfront. A big draw with day-trippers and pre-Christmas bargain hunters.

The Booth Museum of Natural History
Macabre collection of stuffed animals, butterflies and dinosaur bones assembled by eccentric 19th-century naturalist/collector Edward Thomas Booth. Houses some half a million items.
- Dyke Road BN1 5AA
- T (01273) 292777
  www.booth.virtualmuseum.info
- Mon-Sat 10-5, Sun 2-5. Closed Thurs, Good Friday

Brighton Toy and Model Museum
More than 10,000 vintage toys and models – including a priceless train set – are held in this treasure trove of childhood under the arches beneath Brighton Station.
- Trafalgar Street BN1 4EB
- T (01273) 749494
  www.brightontoymuseum.co.uk
- Tue to Fri 10-5, Sat 11-5. Closed Sun and Mon

Brunswick
(see Brighton's Villages, p76, and Other Major Attractions, p41)

iO Gallery Brighton Designers and Make
This eclectic gallery was set up in 1997 to showcase the work of locally based craft workers specialising in everything from glass-working through ceramics to jewellery-making.
- Sydney Street BN1 4EP
- T (01273) 671212
  www.iogallery.co.uk
- Mon to Sat 10-6, Sun 11-5

Kemp Town
(see Brighton's Villages, p80)

North Laine Photography Gallery
With an exhibition space on the first floor of Snoopers' Paradise indoor flea market in Kensington Gardens, this contemporary photography gallery unashamedly focuses on Brighton.
- Kensington Gardens BN1 4AL
- T (01273) 686506
  www.northlainephotography.co.uk
- Daily except over Christmas

www.visitbrighton.com

0906 711 2255*

Architecture, Heritage and Galleries

49

Other Attractions

O Contemporary
This stylish, recently opened gallery near Brighton Station has already showcased work from the biggest names in modern art, including Andy Warhol, David Hockney and Damien Hirst.

i Trafalgar Street BN1 4EB

T (01273) 698500

www.ocontemporary.com

Tue to Fri 105.30, Sat 10-6, Sun 12-5

Permanent Gallery
Another recent addition to Brighton's burgeoning gallery scene, this artist-run, not-for-profit venue also houses an independent art bookshop run by the art collective Borbonesa.

i Bedford Place BN1 2PT

T (01273) 710771

www.permanentgallery.com

Phone for opening times

The Phoenix Arts Association
This contemporary, artist-run gallery boasts extensive exhibition space and one of the few remaining studio complexes in Brighton not to have been converted into luxury apartments.

i Waterloo Place BN2 9NB

T (01273) 603700

www.phoenixarts.org

Phone for opening times

*calls cost 50p per minute, UK only

Royal Pavilion
(see Most Popular Attractions, p34)

Two Kats and a Cow Gallery
A funky, artist-led studio and gallery with gorgeous sea views located right on Brighton beachfront, this is a popular draw among day-trippers and serious art lovers alike.

i Kings Road Arches BN1 1NB

T (01273) 776746

www.twokatsandacow.com

Sat and Sun 11-5, or by appointment

University of Brighton Gallery
This influential gallery in central Brighton is the venue for the university's annual BA and MA degree shows and a rolling programme of photography and fine art exhibitions.

i Grand Parade BN2 0JY

T (01273) 643010

www.brighton.ac.uk/gallery

Mon to Sat 10-5 during exhibitions. Closed Bank Holidays

biggest names in modern art

50 Entertainment

www.visitbrighton.com

The breadth of entertainment available in Brighton and Hove for adults and families alike is breathtaking. Prices listed are approximate and reflect typical ticket costs at time of printing.

⭐ Theatre and Comedy

Brighton and Hove has a long theatrical tradition, with many of the 20th-century's greatest thespians and playwrights having made it their home. Lord Olivier, Sir Terence Rattigan and music hall legend Max Miller are among the stage legends to have lived here. Fittingly, the city today boasts a wide array of performance venues.

Gardner Arts Centre
(see also Cinemas, p52)
The first campus arts centre in the UK, this purpose-built Grade II* listed venue hosts a packed year-round programme. Recent shows have ranged from *The Gruffalo's Child* to comic Mark Thomas.

- University of Sussex, Falmer BN1 9RA
- T (01273) 685861
- www.gardnerarts.co.uk
- £ under £10
- ♿ Good

The Komedia
Brighton's premier fringe venue recently gained a new entrance and foyer bar-cum-performance space. What remains constant are its tasty tapas menu and ever more eclectic live theatre, comedy and music programme.

- 44 Gardner Street BN1 1UN
- T (01273) 647100
- www.komedia.co.uk/brighton/
- £ £10-£20
- ♿ Excellent

Joogleberry Playhouse
With its stylish café and intimate basement cabaret bar, the Joogleberry sent a shot across the Komedia's bows when it opened in 2003. Hosts a packed year-round programme of live theatre, music and comedy.

- 14-17 Manchester Street BN2 1TF
- T (01273) 687171
- www.joogleberry.com
- £ under £10
- ♿ Good

Marlborough Theatre
Housed in a cosy room above the charming Marlborough Tavern, this 50-seater theatre showcases new amateur productions and is an emerging fringe venue during October's Brighton Paramount Comedy Festival. Comes into its own during May festival, when it often previews shows bound for Edinburgh.

- 4 Princes Street BN2 1RD
- T (07782) 278521
- www.marlboroughtheatre.co.uk
- £ under £10
- ♿ Limited

long theatrical tradition

51 Entertainment

0906 711 2255*

New Venture Theatre
Formed in 1947, this fierccly independent community theatre group promoting original work was initially nomadic, but now has its own venue with two performance spaces, including a 100-seater proscenium arch theatre. Promotes original work.
- *i* Bedford Place BN1 2TP
- **T** (01273) 746118
  www.newventure.org.uk
- **£** under £10
- ♿ Good

Nightingale Theatre
Like the Marlborough, this intimate performance space is housed in a room above a pub, in this case the recently refurbished Grand Central opposite Brighton Station. Showcases work of new and emerging writers.
- *i* 29-30 Surrey Street BN1 3PA
- **T** (01273) 702563
  www.nightingaletheatre.co.uk
- **£** Call for details
- ♿ Limited

Sallis Benney Theatre
Recently refurbished, this city-centre venue is being transformed into the University of Brighton's answer to the Gardner Arts Centre, with theatre and comedy slotting into its established literary and music programme.
- *i* University of Brighton, Grand Parade BN2 0JY
- **T** (01273) 709709
  www.brighton.ac.uk/gallery-theatre/
- **£** Call for details
- ♿ Excellent

Theatre Royal
Now owned by Sir Cameron Macintosh's Ambassadors Theatre Group, this handsome Georgian playhouse is Brighton's principal mainstream stage venue. Celebrating its 200th birthday this year (2007), it is said to be haunted.
- *i* New Road BN1 1SD
- **T** (01273) 328488
  www.theambassadors.com/theatreroyal/
- **£** £10-£2
- ♿ Good

*calls cost 50p per minute, UK only

promotes original work

Entertainment

⭐ Cinemas

Brighton has a strong case for being considered the birthplace of cinema. Early pioneers like William Friese-Greene and George Albert Smith lived and worked here, with the latter opening one of the first UK film studios at St Ann's Well Gardens, Hove. Brighton's first screening took place using a cinematograph in 1896 at the Pandora Gallery, opposite the West Pier.

Brighton Cinematheque

Once a cinema in its own right, but now more of an art-house 'club' for serious film-buffs. Its challenging, esoteric programmes are shown at venues including the Nightingale Theatre and the Friends Meeting House.

- **£** Free or under £10
- www.cinematheque.org
- ♿ Good to limited (depending on venue)

Duke of York's Picture-house

Now the city's principal art-house venue, this is the oldest surviving purpose-built cinema in Britain. Opened on 22 September 1910, its debut programme included a film by local pioneer GA Smith, *Byways of Byron*.

- ℹ Preston Circus BN1 4NA
- **T** (01273) 626261
- www.picturehouses.co.uk/cinema
- **£** under £10
- ♿ Good

Gardner Arts Centre

(see also Theatre and Comedy, p50) Brighton's 'other' art-house cinema, this venue on the University of Sussex campus is a 15-minute drive or train journey out of Brighton. Doubles as a major performance space for theatre and comedy.

- ℹ University of Sussex, Falmer BN1 9RA
- **T** (01273) 685861
- www.gardnerarts.co.uk
- **£** under £10
- ♿ Good

Odeon

Opened in 1937, this is the main city-centre destination for filmgoers seeking out the latest Hollywood blockbuster. Recently extended in capacity from six to eight screens, it contains a Haagen Dazs café.

- ℹ Kingswest, West Street BN1 2RE
- **T** (0871) 22 44 007
- www.odeon.co.uk
- **£** under £10
- ♿ Good

Cineworld

This eight-screen multiplex based at Brighton Marina boasts a handy free car park for those driving in from the city centre or suburbs. For the mobile, Brighton's prime destination for mainstream movies.

- ℹ Brighton Marina Village BN2 5UT
- **T** (0871) 200 2000
- www.cineworld.co.uk/
- **£** Call cinema for details
- ♿ Excellent

Picture house DUKE OF YORK'S BRIGHTON

0906 711 2255*

53
Entertainment

⭐ Live Music (major concert venues)

Following a sustained period of refurbishment of its key venues in the late 1990s, Brighton and Hove is now challenging Reading and Guildford as the main pretender to London's crown as the South East's live music capital.

Brighton Centre

Opened in 1977, this 4,500-seater concrete hall, which has hosted many a party conference, remains Brighton's premier live music venue, playing host to numerous international stars each year – from Tom Jones to Blur.

i Kings Road BN1 2GR

T (0870) 900 9100

www.brightoncentre.co.uk

£ varies from £10 to over £20
♿ Excellent

Brighton Dome

This Grade I listed building on the Royal Pavilion estate was once the Prince Regent's stables. Recently refurbished to the tune of £38 million, it incorporates three venues, including the dinky Pavilion Theatre and the cavernous Corn Exchange.

i New Road BN1 1UG

T (01273) 709709

www.brightondome.org

£ £10-£20
♿ Excellent

Concorde 2

Brighton's premier alternative music venue, this is the successor to the cult Concorde bar, which hosted club nights and salsa classes at its base by the Sea Life Centre. Specialises in giving emerging Indie bands a leg up, and introducing 1970s soul-funk acts to a new audience.

i Madeira Drive BN2 1PS

T (01273) 673311

www.concorde2.co.uk

£ up to £20
♿ Good

Glyndebourne Festival Opera

Known for its Pimms and strawberries image, this esteemed venue set in an idyllic location near Lewes has a world-class reputation among opera-lovers. It comes into its own during its summer season, but also boasts an extended winter touring programme.

i Glyndebourne, Lewes BN8 5UU

T (01273) 812321

www.glyndebourne.com

£ varies from under £10 to over £20
♿ Excellent

Old Market

Housed in a recently restored Grade II listed indoor market hall dating back to 1828, the Old Market has a fast-growing reputation as one of the city's most exciting and varied live music and theatre venues.

i 11a Upper Market Street BN3 1AS

T (01273) 736222

www.theoldmarket.co.uk

£ up to £20
♿ Excellent

*calls cost 50p per minute, UK only

Entertainment

⭐ Live Music (Small venues)

Fat Boy Slim, British Sea Power and The Electric Soft Parade: Brighton and Hove has spawned numerous household-name music acts in the past decade – thanks, in part, to the growing number of locally based record labels. The emergence of a Brighton 'scene' has also been reflected in an explosion of smaller live venues, many of them above or below pubs.

The Greys

In keeping with its reputation as Brighton's best gastro-pub, this tiny venue is aimed at connoisseurs who read the credits on record sleeve notes. Attracts some of the world's most talented, if lesser-known, guitarists and singer-songwriters, and has a monthly folk club night.

- *i* 105 Southover Street BN2 9UA
- **T** (01273) 680734
- www.greyspub.com
- **£** £10-£20
- ♿ Limited

The Lion and Lobster

An ever more adventurous live music venue, this hospitable pub near the Brighton-Hove border is best known for its lively Thursday and Sunday jazz nights courtesy of the city's acclaimed Brighton Jazz All-Stars.

- *i* 24 Sillwood Street BN1 2PS
- **T** (01273) 327299
- www.lionandlobster.com
- **£** Free
- ♿ Good

The Pressure Point

Long-standing upstairs pub venue which hosts a mix of home-grown and established talent, as well as local heats of global Battle of the Bands contests. Recent shows have included a gig by rising Indie stars The Kooks.

- *i* 33 Richmond Place BN2 9NA
- **T** (01273) 702333
- www.pressurepoint.me.uk
- **£** under £1
- ♿ Limited

The Prince Albert

Drop by for a pay-on-the-door performance almost any night at this friendly upstairs pub venue near Brighton Station. Specialises in retro-style acts with punk, Goth and 80s electro-pop influences.

- *i* 48 Trafalgar Street BN1 4ED
- **T** (01273) 730499
- www.itchybrighton.co.uk
- **£** Free or under £10
- ♿ Limited

The Sussex Arts Club

With its plush leather armchairs and incredible walk-in marble urinals, this private members' club may seem an unlikely venue for live music. But whether you can afford to stump up the £200 membership fee or not, you'd do well to check out its varied programme of live jazz, global vibes and comedy, which is open to members and non-members alike.

- *i* 7 Ship Street, Brighton BN1 1AD
- **T** (01273) 727371
- www.sussexarts.com
- **£** under £10
- ♿ Good

emergence of a 'Brighton scene'

Entertainment

⭐ Nightclubs

Next to London, Brighton and Hove is the undisputed clubbing capital of the South East. From hard house and hip-hop through 70s funk to Indie and heavy rock, the city has something to cater for every taste.

Audio
A byword for classy dance music, this seafront club scooped Brighton's inaugural Best Bar None award last year (2006).

i 10 Marine Parade BN2 1TL

T (01273) 697775

www.audiobrighton.com

£ under £10
♿ Good

The Beach Club
By day its outdoor patio is a beach bum's delight. At night it's one of Brighton's funkiest dance clubs.

i 171-181 Kings Road Arches BN1 1NB

T (01273) 722272

£ under £10
♿ Good

Casablanca
Live bands play in the basement of this laid-back funk club, furnished with reconditioned Volkswagen Beetle seats.

i 2-5 Middle Street BN1 1AL

T (01273) 321817

www.casablancajazzclub.com

£ Free or under £10
♿ Limited

The Club
Formerly named Envy, this cosy upstairs dance club is one of the city's most popular gay venues (see Gay Brighton, p82).

i 8 Marine Parade BN2 1TA

T (01273) 624091

£ £10-£20
♿ Limited

Club Revenge
Open every night, Brighton's premier gay club offers a rolling programme of themed nights, including men-only events (see Gay Brighton, p82).

i 32-34 Old Steine BN1 1EL

www.revenge.co.uk

£ under £10
♿ Limited

Enigma
Unpretentious and affordable upstairs club which attracts a mixed age range to its varied themed nights.

i 10 Ship Street BN1 1AD

T (01273) 328439

£ under £10
♿ Limited

Funky Buddha Lounge
New York-style twin tunnels lend this chilled-out beachfront dance club an intimate, subterranean feel.

i 169 Kings Road Arches BN1 1NB

T (01273) 725541

www.funkybuddha.co.uk

£ under £10
♿ Good

0906 711 2255*

55

*calls cost 50p per minute, UK only

undisputed clubbing capital of the South East

Entertainment

★ Nightclubs (Continued)

Funky Fish
Aimed at 30-somethings who fancy dancing to old 70s favourites, but recoil at thoughts of Abba.
- 19 Marine Parade BN2 1TL
- T (01273) 698331
- www.funkyfishclub.co.uk
- £ under £10
- ♿ Good

Harlequin
Cheap and cheerful club that offers a winning mix of unpretentious retro tunes and pub prices (see Gay Brighton, p82).
- 43 Providence Place, BN1 4GE
- T (01273) 620630
- www.harlequin-brighton.co.uk
- £ under £10
- ♿ Limited

Honey Club
Popular beachfront dance club with seven bars. A magnet for some of Britain's top DJs.
- 214 Kings Road Arches BN2
- T (07000) 446639
- www.thehoneyclub.co.uk
- £ under £10
- ♿ Good

The Jazz Place
Basement funk club with cult following courtesy of resident DJ Russ Dewbury's legendary Jazz Rooms nights.
- 10 Ship Street BN1 1AD
- T (01273) 328439
- www.jazzbop.co.uk/jazzrooms/
- £ under £1
- ♿ Limited

Ocean Rooms
Stylish club which attracts regular live acts, set back from main seafront drag. Voted Nightclub of the Year in 2003.
- 1 Morley Street BN2 9RA
- T (01273) 699069
- www.oceanrooms.co.uk
- £ under £10
- ♿ Good

Sumo
Beloved of style-conscious students, this late bar-cum-club favours house music and r'n'b.
- 9-12 Middle Street BN1 1AL
- T (01273) 749465
- www.itchybrighton.co.uk
- £ Free or under £10
- ♿ Good

The Tavern Club
An antidote to the hard dance clubs, this fiercely retro venue plays Indie classics from 60s to present day.
- Royal Pavilion Tavern, Castle Square BN1 1FX
- T (01273) 729400
- £ under £10
- ♿ Limited

The Volks Bar and Club
This tiny, no-frills, old-style Brighton beachfront club hosts easygoing reggae and funky hip-hop nights.
- 3 The Colonnade, Madeira Drive BN2 1PS
- T (01273) 682828
- www.volksclub.co.uk
- £ under £10
- ♿ Limited

magnet for some of Britain's top DJs

All photographs credit: Nick Titchner

58
Eating and Drinking

There are numerous opportunities to eat out in style in Brighton and Hove – whatever your budget and culinary preferences. The city is awash with quality eateries, but prices vary enormously, with pubs and cafes tending to be cheaper than restaurants. The following places to eat are graded in order of cost:
£ main courses £10 or less; ££ mains £10-£15; £££ mains £15+.

✴ Cafés

Those in search of a decent frappuccino will be pleased to know Brighton and Hove has its fair share of all the usual chains, from Starbucks to Caffe Nero. But what really marks it out from most other cities is its sheer number and variety of independent outlets.

Bill's (£)
Wholefood deli-cafe renowned for use of high quality fresh ingredients
- The Depot, 100 North Road, BN1 1YE
- T (01273) 692894
  www.billsproducestore.co.uk
- ♿ Good

Bona Foodie (£)
Freshly prepared 'bespoke baguettes' and mouth-watering window display of home-made cakes
- 21St James's Street, BN2 1RF
- T (01273) 698007
- ♿ Good

Brighton Museum and Art Gallery café (£)
Enjoy a cream tea on the recently restored balcony overlooking the museum's decorative art collections
- Royal Pavilion Gardens BN1 1EE
- T (01273) 290900
  www.brighton.virtualmuseum.info/
- ♿ Excellent

The Dumb Waiter (£)
Bohemian café specialising in hearty breakfasts, named after its vintage food lift
- 28 Sydney Street, BN1 4EP
- T (01273) 602526
- ♿ Good

Frank-in-Steine (£)
Converted Art Deco public lavatory overlooking pier. Specialises in doorstep toasties
- Old Steine, BN1 1GY
- T (01273) 674 742
- ♿ Excellent

Fruit Fix (£)
Trendy, minimalist juice outlet resembling the milk bar in A Clockwork Orange
- Bond Street, BN1 1RD
- T (01273) 819492
- ♿ Good

The Guarana Bar (£)
Brazilian-style café without the coffee. specialises in energy-boosting herbal drinks
- 36 Sydney Street, BN1 4EP
- T (01273) 621406
  www.guaranaco.com
- ♿ Good

Komedia café-bar (£)
Licensed café on ground floor of city's recently refurbished Komedia venue
- 44 Gardner Street, BN1 1UN
- T (01273) 647100
  www.komedia.co.uk/brighton/
- ♿ Excellent

eat out in style

www.visitbrighton.com

0906 711 2255*

59
Eating and Drinking

The Mad Hatter (£)
Colourful café and performance venue, specialising in huge range of ciabattas

📍 35 Montpelier Road, BN1 3BA

T (01273) 722279
www.themadhattercafe.co.uk
♿ Good

The Mock Turtle (£)
Egon Ronay-approved teashop, specialising in cream teas and homemade cakes

📍 4 Pool Valley, BN1 1NJ

T (01273) 327380
♿ Limited

Offbeat Coffee Bar (£)
Journey back to the 'Mods and Rockers' era in this friendly retro café

📍 37 Sydney Street, BN1 4EP

T (01273) 604206
♿ Good

Pavilion Gardens Café (£)
Open-air café with unrivalled view of pavilion. Bands and orchestras play on Sundays

📍 Pavilion Gardens, BN1 1UG

T (01273) 73071
www.paviliongardenscafe.co.uk
♿ Excellent

Pokeno Pies (£)
Lauded by national food critics for its huge range of quality homemade pies

📍 52 Gardner Street, BN1 1UN

T (01273) 684921
www.pokeno.co.uk
♿ Good

*calls cost 50p per minute, UK only

Red Roaster (£)
Independent Fair Trade coffee house that roasts beans on the premises

📍 1D St James's Street, BN2 1RE

T (01273) 719526
♿ Excellent

Wild Cherry (£)
Organic, family-run deli-cafe boasting global snack menu in colourful Hanover

📍 91 Queens Park Road, BN2 0GJ

T (01273) 691494
♿ Limited

✱ Pubs/Bars

Brighton and Hove famously boasts more pubs and bars per square mile than virtually any other British city. From traditional boozers to stripped-back, stylish modern bars and acclaimed gastro-pubs, with many now serving a quality range of home-cooked snacks and meals. If you choose to take the car to any of the pubs listed, don't forget to designate a driver who won't be drinking.

The Barley Mow (£)
Kemp Town pub with large rear garden offering huge array of dishes until late evening

📍 92 St George's Road, Kemp Town, BN2 1EE

T (01273) 682259
♿ Good

modern bars and acclaimed gastro-pubs

60
Eating and Drinking

The Basketmakers (£)
Recommended by the Campaign for Real Ale, this traditional pub serves hearty main dishes for under £6
- 12 Gloucester Road, BN1 4AD
- T (01273) 689006
- & Limited

Brighton Rocks (££)
Trendy whitewashed Kemp Town gastro-pub serving quality, affordable modern European tapas menu
- 6 Rock Place, BN2 1PF
- T (01273) 601139
  www.brighton-rocks.com
- & Good

The Cricketers (£)
Reputedly Brighton's oldest pub, the upstairs restaurant is named Greene Room in memory of one-time patron Graham Greene
- 15 Black Lion Street, BN1 1ND
- T (01273) 329472
- & Limited

The Dorset (££)
Elegant North Laine café-bar, specialising in quality breakfasts, seafood and grills at affordable prices
- 28 North Road, BN1 1YB
- T (01273) 605423
  www.thedorset.co.uk
- & Good

The Dover Castle (£)
Friendly pub in residential area serving global dishes
- 43 Southover Street, BN2 9UE
- T (01273) 688276
- & Good

The Eagle Bar and Bakery (£)
Pizzas and bread are baked on the premises, in full view of punters
- 125 Gloucester Road, BN1 4AF
- T (01273) 607765
- & Good

The Earth and Stars (£)
Popular central pub where everything is organic
- 26 Windsor Street, BN1 1RJ
- T (01273) 722879
- & Limited

The Greys (££)
Renowned for encyclopaedic range of Belgian beers and Egon Ronay-approved seasonal menu
- 105 Southover Street, BN2 9UA
- T (01273) 680734
  www.greyspub.com
- & Limited

The John Harvey Tavern (££)
Real ales straight from next-door brewery and daily specials make this Lewes pub well worth a train ride
- Bear Yard, Cliffe High Street, BN7 2AH
- T (01273) 479880
  www.harveys.org.uk
- & Good

The Pond (£)
Authentic Thai dishes make the dining area of this traditional pub one of Brighton's best Asian eateries
- 49 Gloucester Road, BN1 4AQ
- T (01273) 621400
- & Limited

The Ram (££)
Recently refurbished Georgian country pub renowned for posh lunches and à la carte evening menu
- The Street, Firle, near Lewes, BN8 6NS
- T (01273) 858222
- & Good

encyclopaedic range of Belgian beers

0906 711 2255*

61
Eating and Drinking

The Snowdrop (££)
Named after a mini-avalanche from the cliff above, this popular Lewes pub serves food seven days a week

i 119 South Street, Lewes, BN7 2BU

T (01273) 471018
& Good

The Walmer (£)
Colourful Hanover pub known for its huge goldfish tanks and tasty homemade pizzas

i 95 Queen's Park Road, BN2 0GH

T (01273) 682466
& Good

✦ British Restaurants

Brighton and Hove has a growing gastronomic reputation, with all corners of the globe represented somewhere among its myriad fine restaurants. Like every city, it has the usual high street chains, from McDonald's to Kentucky Fried Chicken. But, unlike many, it also boasts a bewildering array of quality independent eateries.

Blanch House (£££)
Surprisingly affordable fine dining restaurant in one of Brighton's most stylish boutique hotels

i 17 Atlingworth Street, BN2 1PL

T (01273) 603504
www.blanchhouse.co.uk
& Limited

Browns Restaurant and Bar (££)
A local institution, this was the first Browns café bar-style restaurant

i 3-4 Duke Street, BN1 1AH

T (01273) 323501
www.browns-restaurants.com
& Good

Due South (£££)
Highly rated (and oft-reviewed) beachfront restaurant committed to sourcing local and seasonal produce

i 139 Kings Road Arches, BN1 2FN

T (01273) 821218
www.duesouth.co.uk
& Limited

Harry's English Restaurant (££)
Wholesome family-run restaurant known for its generous portions of hearty traditional dishes

i 41 Church Road, Hove, BN3 2BE

T (0871) 2071852
www.harrysrestaurant.co.uk
& Good

Hotel du Vin (£££)
Contemporary British cuisine using quality seasonal ingredients served in luxurious setting

i Ship Street, BN1 1AD

T (01273) 718588
www.hotelduvin.com
& Good

Real Eating Company (££)
Informal, 35-seater family-friendly café-cum-restaurant in acclaimed wholefood shop

i 86-87 Western Road, BN3 1JB

T (01273) 221444
www.real-eating.co.uk
& Good

Saucy British Restaurant (£££)
This fine dining, contemporary British restaurant recently opened to rave reviews

i 8 Church Road, Hove, BN3

T (01273) 324080
& Good

*calls cost 50p per minute, UK only

array of quality independent eateries

Eating and Drinking

Seven Dials (£££)
Fine dining restaurant in heart of Brighton's increasingly metropolitan-style Seven Dials district
- 1 Buckingham Place, BN1 3TD
- T (01273) 885 555
  www.sevendialsrestaurant.co.uk
- & Good

The Strand (£££)
Cosy, highly rated English restaurant in central Brighton, popular for romantic candlelit dinners
- 6 Little East Street, BN1 1HT
- T (01273) 747096
  www.thestrandbrighton.co.uk
- & Good

The Tin Drum (££)
Locally based bar-restaurant chain, with four outlets. The first, and most popular, is at Seven Dials
- 95-97 Dyke Road, BN1 3JE
- T (01273) 777575
  www.tindrum.co.uk
- & Good

✪ European Restaurants

Alfresco (££)
Family-run, seafood-specialist Italian beachfront restaurant in palatial Art Deco building overlooking West Pier
- 26 Kings Rd Arches, BN1 2LN
- T (01273) 206 523
  www.alfresco-brighton.co.uk
- & Excellent

Carluccio's (£)
Stylish, glass-sided, Antonio Carluccio café-bar and restaurant recently opened opposite new Jubilee Library
- Unit 1 Jubilee Street, BN1 1GE
- T (01273) 690493
  www.carluccios.com
- & Excellent

Casa Don Carlos (£)
Brighton's most popular and authentic Spanish tapas bar-restaurant, in the heart of The Lanes
- 5 Union Street, The Lanes, BN1 1HA
- T (01273) 327177
- & Limited

Gingerman (£££)
Stylish, intimate modern European restaurant believed by some to be the best in Brighton
- 21a Norfolk Square, BN1 2PD
- T (01273) 326688
  www.gingermanrestaurants.com
- & Good

La Fourchette (£££)
Posh, popular and pricey classic French cuisine served in elegant, high-ceilinged setting
- 105 Western Road, BN1 2AA
- T (01273) 722556
  www.lafourchette.co.uk
- & Good

La Marinade (£££)
Quality contemporary fusion restaurant run by acclaimed chef Nick Lang, who has cooked for Hugh Grant, Madonna and David Bowie
- 77 St Georges Road, BN21EF
- T (01273) 600992
  www.lamarinade.co.uk
- & Good

Mint Restaurant (££)
This restaurant-cum-piano bar in The Lanes offers European and Mediterranean cuisine in cosy surroundings
- 42 Meeting House Lane, BN1
- T (01273) 323824
- & Good

contemporary fusion restuarant

63
Eating and Drinking

Nia Cafe (££)
Café by day, fully fledged candle-lit restaurant at night. Popular for intimate romantic dinners

i 87-88 Trafalgar Street, BN1 4EB

T (01273) 671371
www.niacafe.co.uk

♿ Limited

One Paston Place (£££)
Brighton's most acclaimed restaurant, this fine dining establishment is tucked away inconspicuously on a residential street

i 1 Paston Place, BN2 1HA

T (01273) 606933
www.onepastonplace.co.uk

♿ Good

The Saint (£££)
Offers a quality menu comparable to that of One Paston Place for those on a (slightly) smaller budget

i 22 St James's Street, BN2 1RF

T (01273) 607835
www.thesaintrestaurant.co.uk

♿ Good

African, American and Asian Restaurants

Bali Brasserie (£)
Set inside what appears to be a bland, 1970s residential block, this is actually a highly authentic Malaysian restaurant

i Kingsway Court, First Avenue, BN3 2LR

T (0871) 2071905

♿ Excellent

Blind Lemon Alley (£)
Tucked down an alley, this endearingly lop-sided, low-ceilinged soul food restaurant is your best bet if you can't get in Momma Cherri's

i 41 Middle Street, BN1 1AL

T (01273) 205151

♿ Limited

The China Garden (££)
Pricey but popular Chinese restaurant with its own pianist and Chinese Dragon dances around Chinese New Year

i 88-91 Preston Street, BN1 2HG

T (01273) 325065

♿ Good

Coriander (££)
Acclaimed North African and Latin-influenced deli-restaurant, specialising in seafood and vegetarian dishes

i 5 Hove Manor Parade, Hove Street, BN3 2DF

T (01273) 730850
www.corianderbrighton.com

♿ Good

Gars (££)
Recently opened contemporary Chinese restaurant in The Lanes, described by The Times as 'the best Chinese in town'

i 19 Prince Albert Street, BN1 1HF

T (01273) 321321
www.gars.co.uk

♿ Limited

The Gourmet Burger Kitchen (£)
A spacious outlet next door to Komedia, this serves a huge variety of burgers, and has family-buckets' more style than McDonald's

i 44-47 Gardner Street, BN1 1UN

T (01273) 685895
www.gbkinfo.com

♿ Excellent

*calls cost 50p per minute, UK only

lop-sided, low-ceilinged soul food restaurant

Eating and Drinking

Momma Cherri's Soul Food Shack (£)
Cult American eatery, as featured – and showered with praise – on Gordon Ramsay's Kitchen Nightmares. Booking essential

i 2-3 Little East Street, BN1 1HT

T (01273) 325305
www.mommacherri.co.uk
&. Good

Moshi Moshi (£)
Popular, glass-sided city-centre sushi restaurant beside Brighton Town Hall

i Opticon, Bartholomew Square, BN1 1JS

T (01273) 719195
www.moshimoshi.co.uk/brighton
&. Excellent

Nounou (£££)
Authentic North African restaurant in heart of Kemp Town, with cosy downstairs bar and belly dancing at weekends

i 120 St George's Road, BN2 1EA

T (01273) 682200
www.nounourestaurant.co.uk
&. Good

Symposio Greek Taverna (££)
Authentic Greek taverna serving huge mezzes. Ideal for either family outings or intimate romantic dinners

i 121 Western Road, Hove, BN3 1DB

T (0871) 2072076
&. Good

★ Seafood, Fish (and Chips) Restaurants

Bankers (£)
Traditional fish and chip restaurant, renowned for generous portions of freshly caught fish and chunky homemade chips

i 116a Western Road, BN1 1HA

T (01273) 328267
&. Good

Bardsleys (£)
This no-frills chippie has a nationwide reputation for serving freshly caught fish and seafood at excellent prices. Bring your own wine

i 23-23a Baker Street, BN1 4JN

T (01273) 681256
&. Good

Café Paradiso (££)
Mediterranean-influenced restaurant specialising in seafood in ideal setting – overlooking the moored boats in Brighton Marina

i Alias Hotel Seattle, Brighton Marina, BN2 5WA

T (01273) 665444
www.aliashotels.com
&. Excellent

English's (£££)
Brighton's most celebrated (if expensive) fish restaurant, in the heart of The Lanes

i 28 East Street, BN1 1HL

T (01273) 327980
www.englishs.co.uk
&. Limited

Eating and Drinking

Fruit de Mer (££)
One of Brighton and Hove's newest seafood restaurants, specialising in modern British interpretations of classic fish dishes

i 42 Waterloo Street, BN3 1AY

T (01273) 733733
♿ Good

The Gourmet Fish and Chip Company (£)
Smart, family-friendly eatery that sources fresh fish daily from Grimsby. Popular children's options include gourmet fish fingers

i Walk of Fame, 18 The Waterfront, Brighton Marina, BN2 5WA

T (01273) 670701
www.gourmetfishandchipcompany.com
♿ Excellent

Latin in the Lane (£££)
Classy Italian eaterie famous for Neapolitan-style seafood counter, brimming with freshly caught shellfish

i 10-11 King's Road, BN1 1NE

T (01273) 328672
♿ Good

The Regency (££)
No-nonsense seafront fish restaurant renowned for its fresh, varied and affordable seafood menu

i 131 King's Road, BN1 2HH

T (01273) 325014
www.theregencyrestaurant.co.uk
♿ Good

Riddle and Fins (££)
Praised by the national newspapers, customers sit munching at stools on shared tables in this classy café-cum-restaurant

i 12b Meeting House Lane, BN1 1HB

T (01273) 323008
www.riddleandfinns.co.uk
♿ Limited

Ruby Tates (££)
Recently opened, highly rated champagne and oyster restaurant with high plastic stools and funky décor in Kemp Town

i 40 St James's Street, BN2 1RG

T (01273) 693251
www.rubytates.co.uk
♿ Limited

Vegetarian and Vegan Restaurants
The Vegetarian Society recently named Brighton the number one destination for veggie food in Britain. It's easy to see why:

Bombay Aloo (£)
Quirky Indian buffet restaurant in centre of Brighton with large array of authentic vegetarian-only dishes

i 39 Ship Street, BN1 1AB

T (01273) 776038
www.bombay-aloo.co.uk
♿ Limited

0906 711 2255*

65

*calls cost 50p per minute, UK only

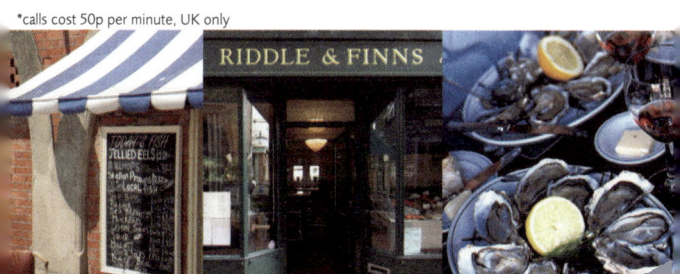

66
Eating and Drinking

Food for Friends (£)
Long-running, stylish and popular eatery in The Lanes (the Terre a Terre for those on tighter budgets)

i 17-18 Prince Albert Street, BN1 1HF

T (01273) 202310
www.foodforfriends.com
♿ Good

Gardenia (£)
Recently established, economical vegetarian restaurant known for its use of fresh natural ingredients

i 2 St James's Street, BN2 1RE

T (01273) 686273
♿ Good

The George (£)
Located a short trot downhill from the train station, this is Brighton's foremost vegetarian gastro-pub

i 5 Trafalgar Street, BN1 4EQ

T (01273) 681055
♿ Good

Planet India (£)
Friendly and economical vegetarian Indian restaurant praised for its use of fresh, authentic ingredients

i 54 Preston Street, BN1 2HE

T (01273) 275717
♿ Good

Planet Janet (£)
Eatery housed in a complementary therapy clinic, with huge menu of vegetarian, vegan and gluten-free options

i 86 Church Road, Hove, BN3 2EB

T (01273) 738389
www.planet-janet.com
♿ Good

Red Veg (£)
This highly rated fast-food burger restaurant was once cruelly described in a review as 'the vegetarian McDonald's'

i 21 Gardner Street, BN1 1UP

T (01273) 679910
♿ Limited

The Sanctuary (£)
Bohemian licensed café with cellar performance venue, specialising in vegetarian/vegan meals and cakes

i 51-55 Brunswick Street East, BN3 1AU

T (01273) 770002
www.sanctuarycafe.co.uk
♿ Limited

Terre a Terre (££)
Brighton's most renowned, if expensive, vegetarian restaurant, it has won numerous awards for its menu and service

i 71 East Street, BN1 1HQ

T (01273) 729051
www.terreaterre.co.uk
♿ Good

Wai Kika Moo Kau (£)
A popular draw for its cosy couches, huge homemade pastries and a varied vegetarian menu

i 11a Kensington Gardens, BN1 4AL

T (01273) 671117
♿ Good

www.visitbrighton.com

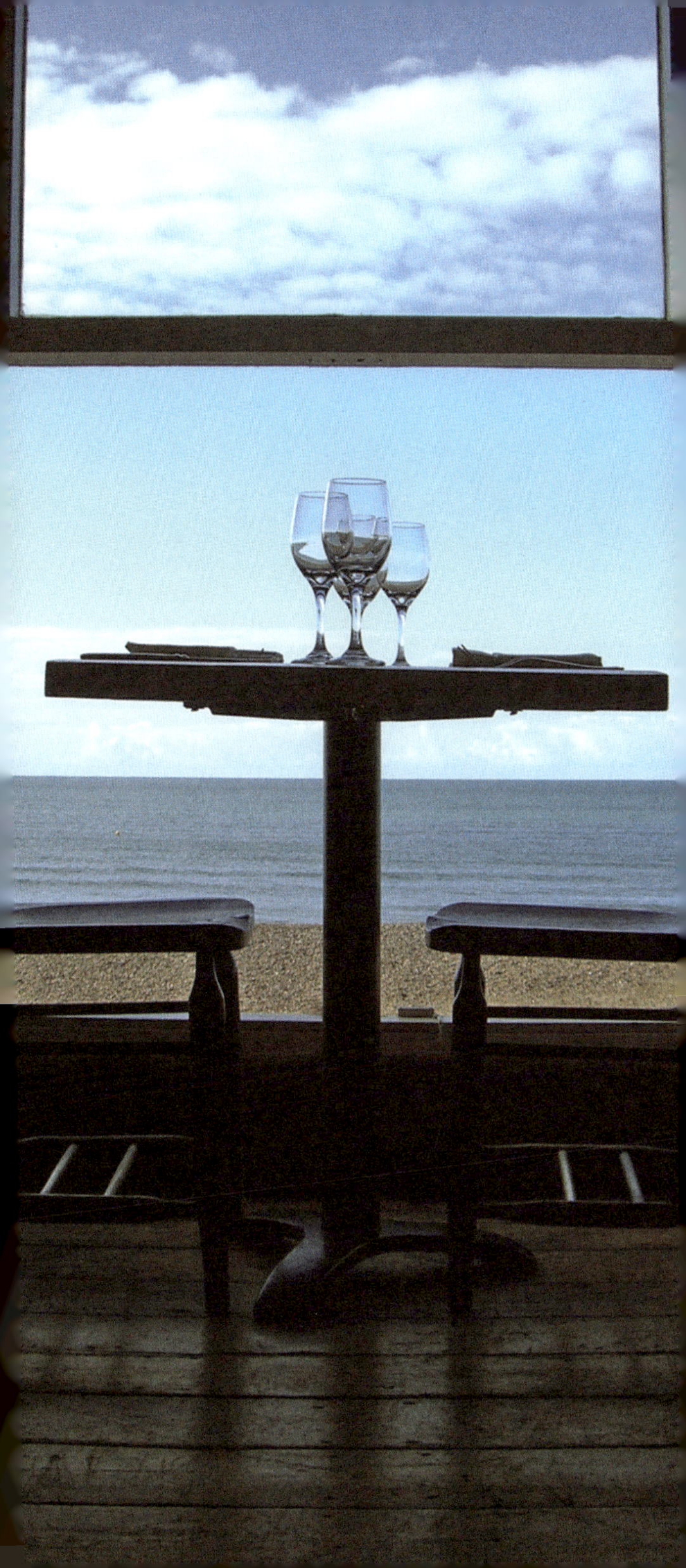

68 Shopping

Brighton Marina Village

Brighton Marina BN2 5UF
T (01273) 818504

www.bmwaterfrontshopping.com

Factory outlets offering designer goods at up to 70% off their usual high street price have turned Brighton Marina into one of the city's most popular shopping destinations. Calvin Klein, Mexx and Bijoux are among the heavily discounted premier brands sold at this Mecca for style-conscious bargain hunters.

Brighton Marina Village has come a long way since the early 1980s, when there was scarcely a shop to be found anywhere within its walls (see Most Popular Attractions, p14). Today, as well as the factory stores, it's home to boutiques galore, an Asda superstore, and smaller shops selling everything from ice cream through books and toys to souvenirs – making it one of the biggest draws in Brighton and Hove for serious shopaholics.

If an afternoon's shopping leaves you a little weary, not to mention hungry, then why not stop by for a latte or cappuccino and a mouth-watering pastry or slice of homemade cake at one of the marina's numerous continental-style cafés?

For those with heartier appetites, the recently opened Boardwalk, with its impressive views over the glistening harbour waters, is a must. Among the popular restaurants jostling for space along this decked walkway are popular grill Ma Potters, the Gourmet Fish and Chip Company and forever-crowded Café Paradiso.

0906 711 2255*

69
Shopping

Brighton Markets

- Brighton Open Market, London Road BN1 4JS
  www.openmarket.org.uk
- Brighton Sunday Market, Trafalgar Street BN1 3XP
- Farmers' markets, George Street, BN3 3YA

There are three principal markets in Brighton – each as individual, quirky and independent-spirited as the other.

Brighton Open Market, off London Road, on the main drag into the city centre for motorists, is a traditional fruit and veg market with an old-style florist, bric-a-brac stands and 'greasy spoon' café. One of its star attractions is ever-friendly fishmonger David Marmery, whose family has run a stall there for the past 73 years. In recent times, the market has diversified, gaining at least one stall specialising in organic produce, and plans are afoot for a £9 million redevelopment by the council.

Another enduring Brighton institution is its popular 'Sunday market' – until recently, a sprawling weekly jumble-cum-antiques sale in the main railway station's car park.

The advent of major redevelopment on that site has seen the size of the market shrink somewhat, but it continues to prove a magnet for bargain-hunters; vinyl-collectors on the lookout for that elusive 45rpm; and students hoping to furnish their new shared house with style – but on a budget.

The most recent addition to Brighton's market scene is a series of periodic farmers' markets and Fair Trade fairs held at Hove's Old Market performance venue.

*calls cost 50p per minute, UK only

70 Shopping

Churchill Square

Western Road BN1 2RG
T (01273) 327428

www.churchillsquare.com

Once a concrete eyesore, Brighton's main covered shopping centre is now an impressive Art Deco-influenced building with an entrance resembling the prow of a pleasure cruiser. The transformation is the result of a £90 million rebuild in the late 1990s.

As with Brighton Marina, Churchill Square is primarily the preserve of major high street brands, with stores like Habitat, HMV, Mothercare, Debenhams, Borders and Next lining the lower and ground floors of its cavernous 470,000sq ft interior. Altogether, the mall is home to more than 85 shops – the majority of which stay open to 7pm on Fridays and Saturdays and 8pm on Thursdays all year round. In addition to the shops themselves, though, it also houses a variety of stalls, selling everything from Italian olives through leather goods to perfume.

On the second floor (accessed by escalator or, for the seriously bag-laden, a lift) a large number of family-friendly restaurants and fast food outlets vie for the custom of 'retailed-out' shoppers.

Churchill Square takes great pains to make an active contribution to the local community, sponsoring charities and holding its own periodic events, such as face-painting workshops for children during school holidays.

impressive Art Deco-influenced building

SQUARE

FIDRA
JEWELLERS

Antiques

72 Shopping

Hove

i Hove BN1 and BN3

i Farmers' markets, George Street, BN3 3YA

Often overlooked by day-trippers in their haste to reach Brighton's picturesque Lanes and seafront, Hove offers more than enough opportunities for retail therapy for serial spendthrifts and casual window-shoppers alike.

Larger outlets, including household names like Waitrose, can be found on the main arterial route running along Western Road and Church Road. More individual outlets, like the numerous small galleries and boutiques and the resolutely independent City Books, which often hosts literary lunches and readings during the Brighton Festival, tend to huddle in the occasional niche or cluster down side streets.

Among Hove's main attractions for shoppers are its large number of antique shops, most of them reasonably priced, and a growing variety of cosmopolitan grocers and delis – from the acclaimed Mediterranean-influenced Coriander through the family-run Real Eating Company to the Japanese Oki Nami store, all of which double as restaurants (see Eating and Drinking, p58).

The city's sole truly pedestrianised shopping street is also located in Hove. The bustling George Street boasts a lively mix of familiar high street names like Boots and WHSmith alongside quirky independent butchers and cafes. Farmers' markets take place there at least once a month, while it also hosts twice-yearly French markets, overflowing with tasty Gallic cheeses, smoked meats and fine wines.

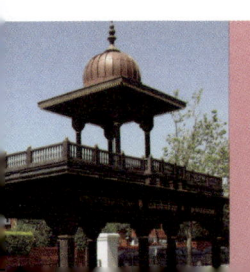

variety of cosmopolitan grocers and delis

www.visitbrighton.com

THE ⟫ L·A·N·E·S →

74
Shopping

The Lanes

The Lanes BN1
(01273) 774000

www.brightonbusiness.co.uk/lbn

The first port of call for many a Christmas shopper in search of that elusive quality stocking-filler, the oldest district in Brighton remains its most historic and popular retail destination.

At the heart of this area, situated five minutes' walk from the seafront, is a series of tight alleys and passageways, crammed with quaint boutiques selling jewellery, antiques, global crafts and all manner of objets d'art (see also Most Popular Attractions, p24). Also nestling among its nooks and crannies is a similarly inviting array of cosy cafes, Victorian tearooms and sweetshops, not to mention several popular pubs and restaurants (see Eating and Drinking).

While the name The Lanes is most closely associated with this central warren of red brick-paved streets, too narrow for vehicle access, the area actually encompasses several peripheral roads too, notably Ship Street and Black Lion Street, location of the historic Cricketers pub (see Eating and Drinking, p60).

Among its most celebrated shops is the evocatively named Choccywoccydoodah, a near-legendary chocolaterie located on Duke Street, whose glorious window displays are, quite literally, chockfull of designer sweets and delicately crafted iced cakes. The shop, which has one sister store in London, employs professional fashion designers and sculptors to produce its multicoloured creations – which resemble everything from trees through statues to furniture.

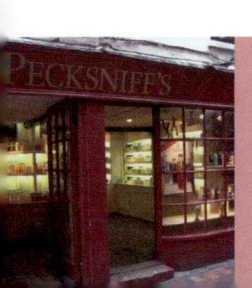

near-legendary chocolaterie

75 Shopping

North Laine

North Laine BN1
T (01273) 601641

www.northlaine.co.uk

Bohemian, cosmopolitan, quirky: Brighton's celebrated North Laine has been called all of these. But, however you choose to describe this half-mile-square sequence of streets meandering from the city's main railway station south towards The Lanes, you're unlikely to find it anything less than memorable (see also Most Popular Attractions, p30).

Regarded as the city's cultural epicentre by many, North Laine boasts nearly 40 cafés, 22 pubs, four theatres, two museums and numerous privately run galleries – not to mention some 300 shops, the majority of them independently owned. With its imaginative, frequently wacky, shop frontages, and even wackier names - *Ju-Ju*, *Pulp Kitchen*, *Cissy Mo* and *Sejuice*, to name a handful – it's no wonder the area is so often likened to Camden in north London.

Not surprisingly, North Laine is a favourite haunt for Christmas shoppers on the lookout for that little something special for a loved one. But nestling among its idiosyncratic craft shops and designer boutiques is a cornucopia of flea markets and second-hand outlets, popular with bookworms and record-collectors. For anyone nostalgic for the era of Mods and Rockers, the area also boasts numerous shops specialising in authentic and reconditioned retro clothing, furniture and household accessories – not to mention iconic Lambretta and Vespa scooters.

*calls cost 50p per minute, UK only

the city's cultural epicentre

76 Brighton's Villages

www.visitbrighton.com

Brunswick

i Brunswick BN3
T (01273) 206306
www.rth.org.uk

This district of panoramic Regency terraces and mews, including Palmeria Square, near the Brighton/Hove border is widely regarded as the jewel in the crown of the city's architectural heritage. The 'wedding cake' splendour of its focal attraction, the Grade I listed Brunswick Square, is recognised as one of the finest examples of Georgian building design anywhere.

Brunswick began life in 1825, when the then colossal sum of £500,000 was invested in a project designed to transform the estate of the Reverend Thomas Scutt. His architect, Charles Augustin Busby, enthusiastically began work on what was to mushroom into a new model town, replete with its own town hall (on Brunswick Street West), market hall, and even, for a time, railway station (on Holland Road).

By the mid-1900s, the glamour of much of Brunswick town had faded, and after the war it became increasingly run-down. As the upkeep of its huge townhouses became too costly for most households, many were gradually acquired by landlords and split into multi-occupancy dwellings.

Since the formation of the Regency Society, in 1945, however, conservationists and the local council have made concerted efforts to protect Brunswick from further development. Their work is celebrated at the newly established Regency Town House (see Other Major Attractions, p41).

★ Highlights

Glorious Grade I listed Regency architecture

Guided tours of Regency Town House museum

Annual Brunswick Festival

BRUNSWICK TERRA

… www.visitbrighton.com

78
Brighton's Villages

Ditchling

Ditchling BN6
www.ditchling.com

Home to a variety of famous residents past and present, this picturesque village lies close to the East/West Sussex border, around seven miles north of Brighton.

From Iron Age settlers via Alfred the Great to 18th-century smugglers, Ditchling has been 'colonised' by all manner of people through the ages. In more recent times, its famously close-knit residents have seen off numerous attempts to alter their largely unspoilt home – including a proposal to build on land sold off by the Abergavenney Estate in 1939, which would have increased Ditchling's population fivefold.

Among the village's most celebrated alumni are the sculptor Eric Gill, who set up a Roman Catholic artistic commune there in 1920, and wartime singer Dame Vera Lynn, who moved there in the 1960s. In 2005, it was the subject of a five-part BBC4 documentary series, A Very English Village, produced by another local resident, filmmaker Luke Holland.

Ditchling's attractions include a museum and two Grade I listed buildings: St Margaret's Church, whose nave dates from the 11th century, and Wings Place, a timber-framed Elizabethan house described in Nairn and Pevsner's survey of Sussex architecture as 'eminently picturesque in a watercolourist's way'.

★ Highlights

Scenic historical village with artistic heritage

Grade I listed church with 11th-century nave

Wings Place Elizabethan house

a very English village

Credit: ianpack.co.uk

Credit: ianpack.co.uk

0906 711 2255*

79
Brighton's Villages

Hanover

i Hanover BN2
T (01273) 694873
www.hanovercommunity.org.uk

With its pastel-coloured Victorian terraces, traditional pubs and artistic reputation, Hanover is one of Brighton's hidden gems. Brunswick is grander and Seven Dials more metropolitan, but the lively yet relaxed atmosphere of this artistic quarter seduces all who visit it.

Hanover's identity as a 'village' distinct from those surrounding it, notably Kemp Town, has emerged gradually over the past two centuries, as the area has expanded and diversified, and word of its charms has spread. In the mid-19th century, it gained its first 'famous' resident: Sir Rowland Hill, designer of the earliest British postage stamp, the Penny Black, who lived at Hanover Crescent.

Today, Hanover is affectionately known as 'muesli mountain', in reference both to its hilly terrain and the high proportion of local residents engaged in liberal professions like teaching and social work. It boasts an active community association; an annual summer street carnival, Hanover Day; a winter beer festival; and more pubs per square mile than virtually any other residential area in England.

Other highlights include Hanover Art Trail (see Brighton Artists' Open Houses, p10), encompassing an annual exhibition by the Brighton Sculptors in the beautiful 19th-century Church of the Annunciation, which has a stained glass window designed by Pre-Raphaelite painter Edward Burne-Jones.

★ Highlights
Patchwork streets of multicoloured terraced houses

Edward Burne-Jones window in Church of the Annunciation

Annual beer festival and street carnival

*calls cost 50p per minute, UK only

one of Brighton's hidden gems

Credit: ianpack.co.uk

80 Brighton's Villages

www.visitbrighton.com

Kemp Town

- Kemp Town BN2
- T (01273) 297088
- www.kemptown-village.co.uk

Along with Brunswick, Kemp Town is arguably the most architecturally striking of Brighton's villages – a fact attributed to the guiding hand of Charles Augustin Busby, the designer responsible for both developments.

The origins of modern Kemp Town date back to 1808, when J B Otto, a West Indian speculator, paid for the construction of Royal Crescent, an islanded development to the east of Brighton's centre. Known for its distinctive black-tiled facades, this showy mews initially outraged local gentry – not least because of the unflattering statue of King George III erected in its gardens, now long since removed.

A little later, Thomas Read Kemp, property developer and MP for Lewes, formulated the idea of building an opulent, planned estate in the same area. Designed by Busby and fellow architect Amon Wilde, this provided the foundation of today's Kemp Town. A further flurry of vanity building followed in the early 1900s, when Sir Albert Sassoon, a friend of King George VII, built his family mausoleum in Preston Place.

Long known as Brighton's principal 'gay quarter' (see Gay Brighton, p82), Kemp Town has boasted numerous 'celebrity' residents, from Lewis Carroll to Ozzy Osbourne. The late Lord Olivier lived on Royal Crescent, while Hollywood actress Cate Blanchett has a home in the stunning Sussex Square.

★ Highlights

Sweeping Regency squares and crescents

Brighton's main 'gay quarter'

Colourful history and celebrity associations

0906 711 2255*

81

Brighton's Villages

Rottingdean

ℹ Rottingdean BN2
www.rottingdean.uk.com

A natural pond that has been a centre of activity since Saxon times and a mention in the Domesday Book are among the early claims to fame of this picturesque fishing village located three miles east of Brighton city centre.

Though signs of habitation date back as far as the Neolithic period, Rottingdean first came to prominence in the late 19th and early 20th centuries, when it became associated with a succession of literary and artistic figures, who found solace in its picture-book charms. Edward Burne-Jones, Angela Thirkell and Rudyard Kipling all moved into stately houses surrounding its focal pond and village green (see Kipling's Garden, p87).

Another famous resident was Kipling's cousin, Stanley Baldwin, later to become Conservative Prime Minister.

These days, Rottingdean has expanded into a ribbon of identikit seafront suburbs, including Saltdean and Peacehaven, stretching eastward as far as Seaford. But the village itself still offers a welcome break for those seeking a brief respite from the bustle of central Brighton. Cream teas and homemade cakes are a speciality of its numerous olde-worlde tea shops, while you can easily spend an afternoon pottering around its quaint gift and antique shops, or strolling along its impressive Undercliff.

★ Highlights
Pretty seaside village
Bracing Undercliff walk
Kipling's Garden

*calls cost 50p per minute, UK only

picturesque fishing village

Credit: janpack.co.uk

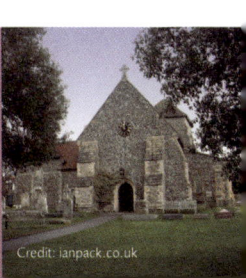

Credit: janpack.co.uk

82

www.visitbrighton.com

Gay Brighton and Hove

Frequently described as the 'gay capital of Britain', Brighton and Hove is one of the most sexually diverse and open cities in the country.

The city has transformed in the last few decades but, for much of the 20th century, it struggled to shake off a reputation as a seedy hideaway for philandering husbands on dirty weekends with their mistresses. But by the late 1960s, it was no longer the preserve of errant Mr and Mrs Smiths, as the escalating sexual revolution – coupled with the decriminalisation of homosexuality – saw it transform into a symbol of the growing sense of personal liberation.

Brighton's 'risque' image dates back to the 19th century, and the saucy antics of the serially unfaithful Prince Regent.

An early story relating to its gay associations concerns philanthropist Angela Burdett-Courts, a friend of Charles Dickens, who regularly stayed at the seafront Royal Albion Hotel with her companion, Hannah. In certain social circles, it was well known that the couple (who sent joint Christmas cards) were an item.

Today, Brighton boasts the highest proportion of gay, lesbian, bisexual and transgender (GLBT) residents in the UK. Recent surveys suggest some 35,000 local people are gay – equivalent to 13% of the overall population, or twice the national average.

★ Living

As the statistics suggest, Brighton and Hove's gay, lesbian, bisexual and transgender community is an essential component of the character of this forever-changing, always vibrant city.

While once GLBT Brightonians, though tolerated, were largely expected to keep themselves to themselves, today such prejudices have been all but vanquished, and there are no longer any 'gay ghettos'. That said, if one particular district remains most closely associated with the gay community it is Kemp Town (see Brighton Villages, p80).

Originally conceived as a gentrified seaside resort by Thomas Read Kemp, 19th-century MP for Lewes, by the mid-1900s Kemp Town had become

Credit: www.realbrighton.com

Credit: www.realbrighton.com

0906 711 2255*

83
Gay Brighton and Hove

more down-at-heel, its handsome townhouses split into low-rent multi-occupancy dwellings. Today it is an altogether smarter quarter, whose cheap guesthouses and greasy-spoon cafes are slowly being transformed into upmarket hotels and restaurants. This concerted facelift is indicative of its increasingly affluent, metropolitan population – the journalist and writer Simon Fanshawe is among the area's most prominent gay residents.

In an effort to recognise the sustained contribution made by the GLBT community to Brighton, the Green Party recently proposed the introduction of plaques commemorating the city's most famous gay residents. Names mooted include former Brighton residents Terence Rattigan, the playwright who penned the script for the film of Graham Greene's Brighton Rock, illustrator Aubrey Beardsley, and his friend, Oscar Wilde, who often stayed at the Royal Albion Hotel.

✣ Clubbing

Flamboyant, energetic and often outrageously camp: Brighton and Hove's gay clubbing scene can be all of these things. But, as the city's GLBT population has grown in size and social diversity, so too has the range of clubs and theme nights extended to cater for ever more varied tastes.

Brighton's most celebrated gay nightspot is the near-legendary Club Revenge (see Entertainment, p55), located a two-minute walk from the seafront. In recent years, though, a number of challengers have emerged to vie for its crown, among them The Club (see p55), a small but popular dance venue located above Charles Street pre-club bar, Zanzibar, and The Harlequin (see p56), an endearingly retro haunt beloved of those who prefer cheesy 70s disco to frenetic drumbeats.

Of the individual club nights, the most famous is undoubtedly Wild Fruit, a celebratory monthly extravaganza held at Creation, in the heart of Brighton's West Street clubbing zone. Here punters, sometimes quite literally, let it all hang out. A favourite on the lesbian scene is the Candy Bar whilst a recent addition is Angels. Held on the first Thursday of each month at the Toad at the Picturehouse, a converted cinema on East Street, it offers drag cabarets, amateur erotic strip shows and hardcore clubbing.

*calls cost 50p per minute, UK only

Credit: www.realbrighton.com

Credit: www.realbrighton.com

Gay Brighton and Hove

⭐ Eating and Drinking

With their refreshingly anything-goes attitudes, few if any of Brighton's 'gay bars' feel exclusive – meaning everyone tends to feel welcome, regardless of sexual orientation.

Among the most popular of Kemp Town's numerous gay watering holes is The Bulldog, a lively pub with a colourful, four-storey façade on St James's Street, offering an unlikely mix of real ale and cabaret. Charles Street Bar and Amsterdam Bar, both on Marine Parade, are perpetually packed pre-club venues. The area's premier gastro-pub is Brighton Rocks (See Eating and Drinking, p59), a funky whitewashed bar on Rock Place, a pebble's throw from the sea.

While all the above are located in Kemp Town, some of the city's most idiosyncratic gay pubs can actually be found some distance away. The Regency Tavern, on Russell Square, sports fabulously kitsch décor – with lovingly preserved 19th-century fittings sitting alongside the golden cherubs adorning the bar and the glitter-balls hanging in the toilets. The seafront Dr Brighton's (named after Dr Richard Russell, see p7) was a favourite haunt of Graham Greene, while The Marlborough Tavern, on Princes Street, boasts an upstairs theatre.

⭐ Celebrating

One of the undisputed highlights of the city's calendar is its annual Brighton Pride event – a wonderfully extravagant, Mardi Gras-style celebration which transforms the centre into one giant party zone for the best part of a weekend each August.

A record 120,000 revellers (equivalent to half the population of Brighton and Hove) lined the streets for a 'Carry On Pride' carnival procession last year (2006), with 70,000 at any one time crowding Preston Park for its climactic live music concert. The 'pink pound' boosted the city's economy by some £5.5 million over the weekend, and stars spotted on the march included, appropriately, Carry On veteran Barbara Windsor.

While Pride is Brighton's biggest gay institution, the city is fast gaining a reputation as the number one destination for GLBT couples seeking to 'marry'. On 5 December 2005, it became the first place in Britain to host a gay civil partnership ceremony, when local resident Matthew Roche was granted special dispensation to marry partner Christopher Cramp, within hours of the law changing.

The city has since hosted numerous other 'gay weddings'. Some 400 couples had applied to marry in Brighton by the time the Civil Partnership Act became law, and three ceremonies were performed simultaneously on the first day they became technically legal, 21 December 2005.

Credit: www.realbrighton.com

Credit: www.realbrighton.com

Credit: www.realbrighton.com

86 Gardens

Borde Hill Garden

- Balcombe Road, Haywards Heath RH16 1XP
- T (01444) 450326
- www.bordehill.co.uk
- Jan to Oct 10-6 daily

Located a short drive outside Haywards Heath, and some 20 minutes from Brighton, this idyllic 17-acre country garden is rightly lauded as one of the most exotic in the UK.

Radiant spring displays of rhododendrons, azaleas, camellias and magnolias blossom alongside flowers more usually found in the climatic extremes of the Himalayas and the tropics. Alongside them flourish plants from as far afield as China, Tasmania, the Andes and North America.

The extraordinarily rich assemblage of flora in the grounds of Borde Hill House is the legacy of Victorian botanist Colonel Stephenson Clarke, who made his home at the Grade II listed Tudor mansion in 1893. He was a generous patron of some of the great 'plant hunters' of his time, inviting them to source ever more extravagant blooms for his magnificent 'living garden rooms' – a series of formal segregated areas encapsulated within 150 acres of sprawling parkland.

Among the most striking attractions of today's Borde Hill estate are the tranquil Garden of Allah; a series of elegant Victorian greenhouses, including one dedicated to the wild blossoms of Africa; the sub-tropical Dells; and a beautiful azalea ring, which explodes into a riot of colour during the summer months.

★ Highlights
Garden of Allah
Victorian greenhouses housing blooms from around the globe
Colourful azalea ring

Information
- Tearoom
- Excellent
- £ Moderate

0906 711 2255*

87
Gardens

Kipling's Garden

i The Green, Rottingdean
BN2 7HA

www.brighton-hove.gov.uk

❋ Open all year round, times vary

Located in the heart of Rottingdean, this fairytale walled garden is named after the most celebrated resident of the pretty fishing village – Rudyard Kipling, author of *The Jungle Book*. Kipling's Garden has been open to the public since 1986, when it was handed into the custodianship of Brighton and Hove Council by the Rottingdean Preservation Society. Three years earlier, the society had bought it for £50,000 from the trustees of the late Lady Jones, in an effort to stop developers building seven new homes on the site, which lies almost at the exact geographical centre of the village.

The Kipling associations date back to 1897, when the writer moved into his Rottingdean home, The Elms, to be near his aunt, Georgina Burne-Jones, wife of painter Sir Edward Burne-Jones, who lived at nearby North End House. While in Rottingdean, he wrote some of his most celebrated fiction, including *Kim* and many of the *Just So Stories*.

Today, the dinky Kipling garden, which is a mere one and a quarter acres in size, has a small croquet lawn and is surrounded by high flint walls. It is bisected by paths constructed during its 1980s renovation using some 30,000 bricks from the neighbouring Dean Court Road.

★ Highlights
Pretty garden in heart of picturesque coastal village
Rudyard Kipling's home village

i Information
♿ Excellent
£ Free/inexpensive

*calls cost 50p per minute, UK only

fairytale walled garden

88 Gardens

Leonardslee Lakes and Gardens

Lower Beeding, Horsham, RH13 6PP
(01403) 891212
www.leonardsleegardens.com

April to Oct 9.30-6 daily (last admission 4.30pm)

Home to wallabies, deer and one of the finest collections of Victorian motor cars in the world, there is far more to Leonardslee than mere plants and flowers. But with 240 sprawling acres of parkland to its name, this scenic estate in Lower Beeding, near Horsham, can certainly give rivals a run for their money in the garden stakes too.

'Modern' Leonardslee was established in 1889 by Sir Edmund Loder, who imported a herd of wallabies that continues to roam the grounds to this day. He embarked on an ambitious woodland garden project, inspired by the planting ideas of pioneers such as Sir Uvedale Price, Richard Payne Knight and J C Loudon.

With seven lakes and a bounteous seasonal riot of rhododendrons and azaleas, Leonardslee offers a picture postcard backdrop for romantic spring strolls and leisurely picnics. Its signature bloom is the aptly named Loderi King George, a flamboyant variety of rhododendron with huge leaves, which flares into fragrant, funnel-shaped, pure white flowers.

Other attractions beside the flora include a collection of eight lovingly maintained Victorian motor vehicles, all manufactured between 1880 and 1990, and a one-twelfth scale model of the Leonardslee estate as it was a century ago.

★ Highlights
Glorious rhododendron displays
Vintage motor museum
Miniature scale model of estate

Information
Restaurant
Good
£ Expensive

home to wallabies, deer ... and motor cars

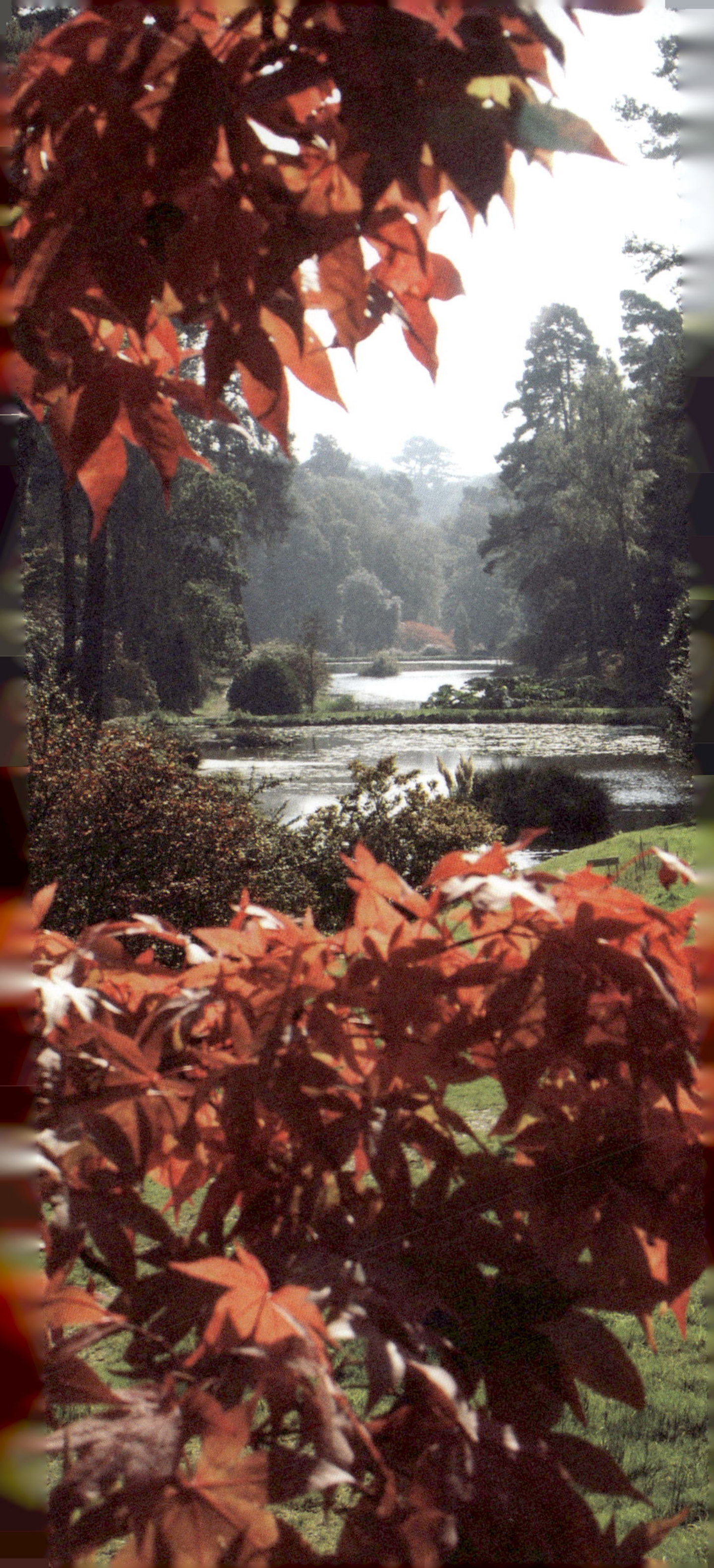

Gardens

Nymans Garden

- Handcross, nr Haywards Heath RH17 6EB
- (01444) 400321
- www.nationaltrust.org.uk
- Mid-Feb to October 10-6, November to Mid-Feb 11-4

The crowning achievement of three generations of the Messel family, Nymans Garden, near Haywards Heath, boasts an internationally renowned collection of rare plants. Bequeathed to the National Trust in 1953, Nymans was one of the first gardens to be taken into the charity's care. In the decades since, its exquisite floral displays, sculpted hedges and breathtaking views have combined to make it one of the most popular outdoor attractions in West Sussex.

Nymans' singular selling point is its effortless marriage of the grandeur of a formal garden with a sense of privacy, courtesy of a series of intimate, screened-off spaces.

Set 500ft up the side of a valley, the 30-acre garden boasts showy views over the Downs from its upper terrace. But at lower levels lie a quaint gazebo frequented by doves, and the oldest single feature: a fairytale walled garden entered via an ornate Italian arch.

Exotic species of plant hail from the four corners of the globe, with South America, the Far East and Tasmania all represented in bright bursts of colour. Among the other curiosities are the ruins of the house itself – a pastiche of a 14th-century manor built for Ludwig Messel in the early 1900s.

★ Highlights
- Sweeping gardens intercut with intimate 'garden rooms'
- Panoramic views over Sussex
- Picture postcard ruins of 14th-century manor house

Information
- Café
- Good
- £ Moderate

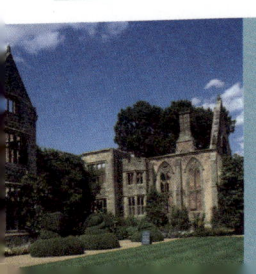

renowned plant collection

0906 711 2255*

91
Gardens

Preston Park

- Preston Road BN1 6RF
- T (01273) 292060
- www.brighton-hove.gov.uk
- Open all year, 24 hours

Brighton's first, biggest and still most popular planned park, this sprawling expanse of green around a mile north of the centre hosts many of the signature outdoor events in the city's calendar – from its main Bonfire Night fireworks display to the annual Pride concert.

Previously part of the Preston Manor estate, the park was sold in 1883 by its owner, William Bennett-Stanford, to the then local authority, the Brighton Corporation, for £50,000. With the help of a generous £70,000 bequest from a local bookmaker, William Edmund Davies, it was lovingly transformed into the well-kept public amenity it is to this day.

Nowadays, as you wander along its long, linear paths, you are as likely to pass rollerbladers or hippies practising T'ai Chi as you are promenading couples or pram-pushing mothers. But in the park's elegant architectural features – notably its imposing clock tower and idiosyncratic Edwardian Rotunda tearooms – there remain charming reminders of yesteryear.

Set at the head of a circular pond, bordered by a rose garden, the Rotunda is a fine example of Modernism, evoking the pavilion-style café designs common in 1920s continental Europe. The Rookery Rock Garden bursts with twisting walkways, streams and waterways contrasting with the landscaped picnic areas, children's playgrounds and tennis courts.

★ Highlights
Brighton and Hove's largest urban park
Tennis courts, bowling green and play areas

i Information
🍽 Cafés
♿ Excellent
£ Free/inexpensive

*calls cost 50p per minute, UK only

idiosyncratic Edwardian Rotunda tearooms

92 Gardens

Sheffield Park Garden

- Sheffield Park TN22 3QX
- (01825) 790231
- www.nationaltrust.org.uk

- Opening times seasonal, phone for details

Boasting a mention in the Domesday Book and landscaping by 'Capability' Brown, this 200-acre country estate is one of the most impressive in Sussex.

Though its origins lie way back in early Medieval times, the first detailed records pertaining to the estate date to August 1538, when its then owner, Thomas Howard, third Duke of Norfolk, entertained Henry VIII. By 1700, its long-established deer park was in the process of being formalised by Lord De La Warr, who laid out lawns and planted an avenue of trees, radiating from the house. This gradual 'taming' of the grounds was to continue throughout the 18th century, but by 1781 Baron Sheffield was enlisting the architect James Wyatt to re-fashion the house in the Gothic style and 'Capability' Brown to landscape the gardens in a less formal vein.

Brown's transformation was to prove the most enduring. Introducing irregular clumps of trees and haphazard paths through the woods pock-marking the grounds, he lent it an air of wildness at odds with its earlier symmetry. Later, some order returned, with the third Earl of Sheffield's introduction of a cricket field, which hosted the first match between England and Australia. Among those playing on the day was one W G Grace.

★ Highlights
Grounds landscaped by 'Capability' Brown
Location of first ever England–Australia cricket match

Information
- Café
- Good
- £ Moderate

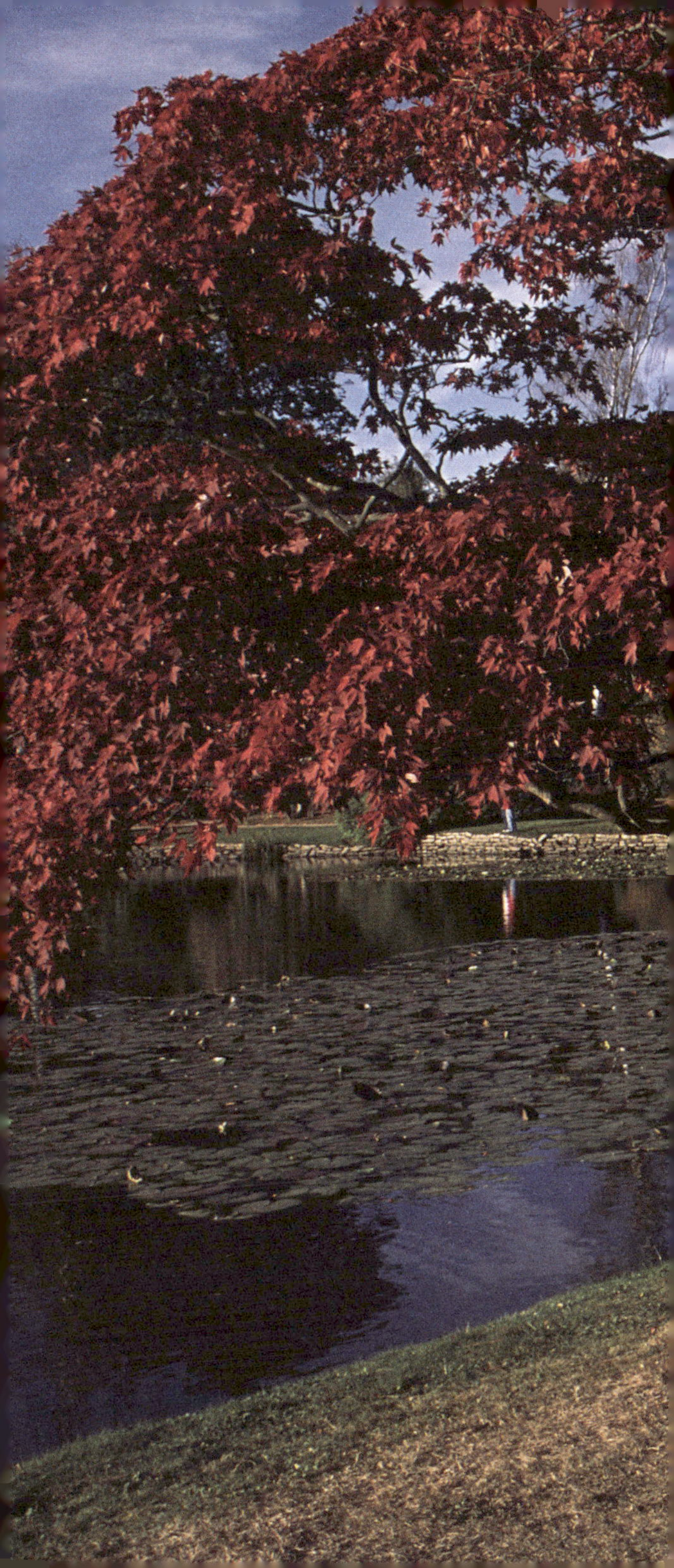

94
Gardens

Stanmer Park

i Lewes Road BN1 9QA
T (01273) 292060
www.brighton-hove.gov.uk

✻ Open all year round, 24 hours

This Grade II listed, landscaped park on the outskirts of Brighton seems to loom out of nowhere as you head out of the city towards the A27. Surrounded by dense woods, its gently undulating slopes offer a foretaste of the sweeping Sussex Downs beyond.

Open to the public throughout the year, Stanmer Park is a popular destination for picnicking families and ramblers alike. One of the most peculiar features of the Stanmer estate is the secluded agricultural village located in it. With its chocolate-box high street, replete with quaint stone cottages, steepled church and duck pond, Stanmer was, quite literally, a private concern until purchased for the people of Brighton in 1947. Even now, shrouded by trees and tucked away in the furthermost corner of the park, stumbling upon it can make you feel as if you had stepped through a crack in time.

The park's other major draw is Stanmer House, a recently restored Grade I listed manor which has become an exclusive wedding venue for well-heeled couples since being leased by Brighton and Hove Council to the multimillionaire tycoon Mike Holland in 2004. This handsome, curiously asymmetrical, building was once home to the Pelham family (not to mention one of the Prince Regent's many mistresses).

★ Highlights
Huge expanse of open parkland
Picture postcard private village
Grade I listed manor house

i Information
♿ Excellent
£ Free/inexpensive

Credit: ianpack.co.uk

0906 711 2255*

95
Gardens

Wakehurst Place

i Ardingly, near Haywards Heath RH17 6TN

T (01444) 894000

www.nationaltrust.org.uk

✤ March to Oct 10-6, Nov to Feb 10-4.30. Closed Christmas Eve & Christmas Day

Now administered by the Royal Botanic Gardens at Kew, Wakehurst Place, in Ardingly, near Haywards Heath, has earned a worldwide reputation for its groundbreaking conservation work.

The estate's associations with plants and, more specifically, the humble herb date back to the Medieval period, when it was occupied for many years by a main branch of the Culpepers, the family credited with pioneering herbalism. Today it is home to the famous Millennium Seed Bank, a repository of some 4,500 plant varieties. It is widely recognised as the biggest botanical conservation project in the world and, by 2010, aims to have collected some 10 per cent of the world's seed-bearing flora. Wakehurst also boasts two unique nature reserves: Loder Valley, which embraces woodland, meadowland and wetland habitats, and Francis Rose, thought to be the first one dedicated to mosses, liverworts, lichens and ferns anywhere in Europe.

As well as its 500 acres of gardens, Wakehurst Place boasts an intriguingly hybrid manor house. Built in 1590 for Edward Culpeper, it underwent numerous alterations over subsequent centuries, not least under one Dennis Lydell, a Royal Navy commissioner and friend of the diarist Samuel Pepys. Its latest addition is a new 'science and learning zone'.

★ Highlights

Millennium Seed Bank containing 4,500 plant varieties
500 acres of gardens
Idiosyncratic 400-year-old manor house

i Information

🍽	Restaurant
♿	Excellent
£	Expensive

*calls cost 50p per minute, UK only

96
Walking

Beachy Head to Belle Toute Lighthouse and Back

Distance: Walk approximately 3 miles (5km)
Time: 2 hours (round trip, including stop)

Start Point: Beachy Head Visitor Centre
End Point: Belle Toute Lighthouse
Lunch: The Beachy Head, Beachy Head Road, Beachy Head (01323) 728060

Starting from one of the most famous landmarks in south-east England, this leisurely three-mile circular stroll follows a gently undulating stretch of coastline westward to the location of the quirky Belle Toute Lighthouse.

With its plunging 300ft cliffs and iconic, sea-level red-and-white working lighthouse, Beachy Head is one of the most-visited sights on the south coast. Readily accessible from the A27 by car or bicycle, and served by frequent buses, on a clear day it is the perfect spot for a picnic, offering breathtaking, uninterrupted views over the sweep of the English Channel.

If you fancy a little modest exercise, why not leave your car at the pay-and-display car park beside the main visitor centre and follow the cliff-top coastal path westwards towards Belle Toute? Located near the site of an earlier wooden lighthouse built by the legendary 'Mad Jack Fuller', the present-day squat, brick-built affair was put up in the 1830s to direct sea traffic safely around this potentially perilous stretch of coast.

The only British lighthouse still used as a permanent home, Belle Toute was hauled 50ft inland in 1999 to save it from tipping off the crumbling cliffs below. It was famously used as a location for the 1980s TV drama *The Life and Loves of a She-Devil*, starring Dennis Waterman.

★ Highlights

Sweeping views over English Channel and Sussex coast

Bracing coastal walk to only lighthouse home left in Britain

Credit: ianpack.co.uk

98 Walking

Brighton and Hove City Centre Guided Walks

Distance: Various
Time: Various
Start Point: Various
End Point: Various
Lunch: Various

www.brightonwalks.com
www.visitbrighton.com

Among the most popular walks in and around Brighton and Hove are its various city centre tours. Some of these are seasonal or periodic rambles led by qualified tour guides, while others take the form of self-directed MP3 walks available for purchase, hire or download.

Brighton-based tour guide Glenda Clarke offers a wide range of themed walks around the city centre, including a popular monthly Ghost Walk, which takes in various landmarks including the Royal Pavilion and the Theatre Royal; a tour of notorious murder scenes; and a Rich, Famous and Infamous Walk, which passes by the former homes and haunts of celebrated former residents such as Charlie Chaplin, Max Miller, Albert Finney and Dames Anna Neagle and Flora Robson.

During the Brighton Festival, several other guided walks regularly take place, including a Brighton Rock tour starting at Brighton Pier, and explorations of the city's extensive network of Victorian sewers.

For those who prefer to explore under their own steam, three MP3 or CD tours are now available, covering the historic Lanes, the area around the Royal Pavilion, and North Laine and Regency Brighton. All can be bought from Tourist Tracks, a company set up by former journalist Tim Gillett; hired from the Visitor Information Centre or downloaded from www.visitbrighton.com

★ Highlights

Expert history lessons on Brighton and Hove's colourful past

User-friendly walking tours of city's glorious Regency architecture

rich, famous and infamous

0906 711 2255*

99
Walking

Devil's Dyke through Fulking to Poynings and Back

Distance: Walk approximately 5 miles (8 km)
Time: 3-4 hours (round trip, including stop for lunch)
Start Point: Summit of Devil's Dyke

End Point: Poynings
Lunch: Shepherd and Dog, The Street, Fulking (01273) 857382 or Royal Oak, The Street, Poynings (01273) 857389

On a bright summer's day, there are few more pleasant ways to spend an afternoon than to catch an open-topped vintage bus from Brighton seafront up to Devil's Dyke and, from there, follow a plunging path down to the scenic conservation village of Fulking.

After taking your fill of the sweeping sea views from the top of the vast valley, whose summit stands 712ft above sea-level, follow the winding, chalky footpath down past flocks of gambolling sheep and clusters of wild flowers towards Fulking, which is listed in the Domesday Book. Within 25 minutes you'll find yourself in the spacious rear garden of the Shepherd and Dog pub, which serves tasty, affordable snacks and light meals.

A further 20-minute walk along the road to nearby Poynings and you can certainly justify a well-earned refreshment break at the Royal Oak, a popular gastro-pub serving a mix of traditional 'pub grub' staples, seasonal specials and more refined, nouvelle cuisine-style dishes.

Don't eat too much, though: if you're aiming to head back up to the top of the dyke afterwards, the climb can seem a good deal more arduous on a full stomach. Beware too that the last number 77 bus back into Brighton leaves at 8.30pm prompt.

★ Highlights

Panoramic views of South Downs and Sussex coast

Plunging walk down to picturesque villages of Fulking and Poynings

*calls cost 50p per minute, UK only

100 Walking

www.visitbrighton.com

Ditchling Beacon to Jack and Jill Windmills and back

Distance: Walk approximately 6 miles (10 km)
Time: 4 hours (round trip, including brief stop)

Start Point: National Trust car park, Ditchling Beacon
End Point: Jill Windmill
Lunch: The Bull, 2 High Street, Ditchling (01273) 843147

This bracing circular walk will take you from the highest point in East Sussex (and third highest on the South Downs) westwards to the lovingly restored Jill windmill and its 'twin' heritage attraction, Jack.

Located some 814ft above sea-level, Ditchling Beacon is the site of an early Iron Age hill-fort, and commands spectacular panoramic views across the forested land to the north of the county. A six-mile drive from Brighton, the beacon has a free National Trust car park, allowing you to explore its environs at your leisure.

Following the hilltop path westwards from the beacon, it is a three-mile walk to the hamlet of Clayton and its twin attractions, the Jack and Jill windmills. The first of the two to be built, Jill, was originally known as Lashmar's New Mill when it was erected to grind corn on the outskirts of Brighton in 1821. It was later moved to Clayton when its land was acquired for development, and there joined by Jack (constructed out of the remains of another, earlier, mill called Duncton).

According to popular belief, the nicknames Jack and Jill were first applied to the mills in the 1920s by day-trippers visiting the area from London.

★ Highlights

Sweeping views of Downs from highest point in East Sussex

Bracing walk to recently restored Jill windmill and 'brother' Jack

early Iron Age hill-fort

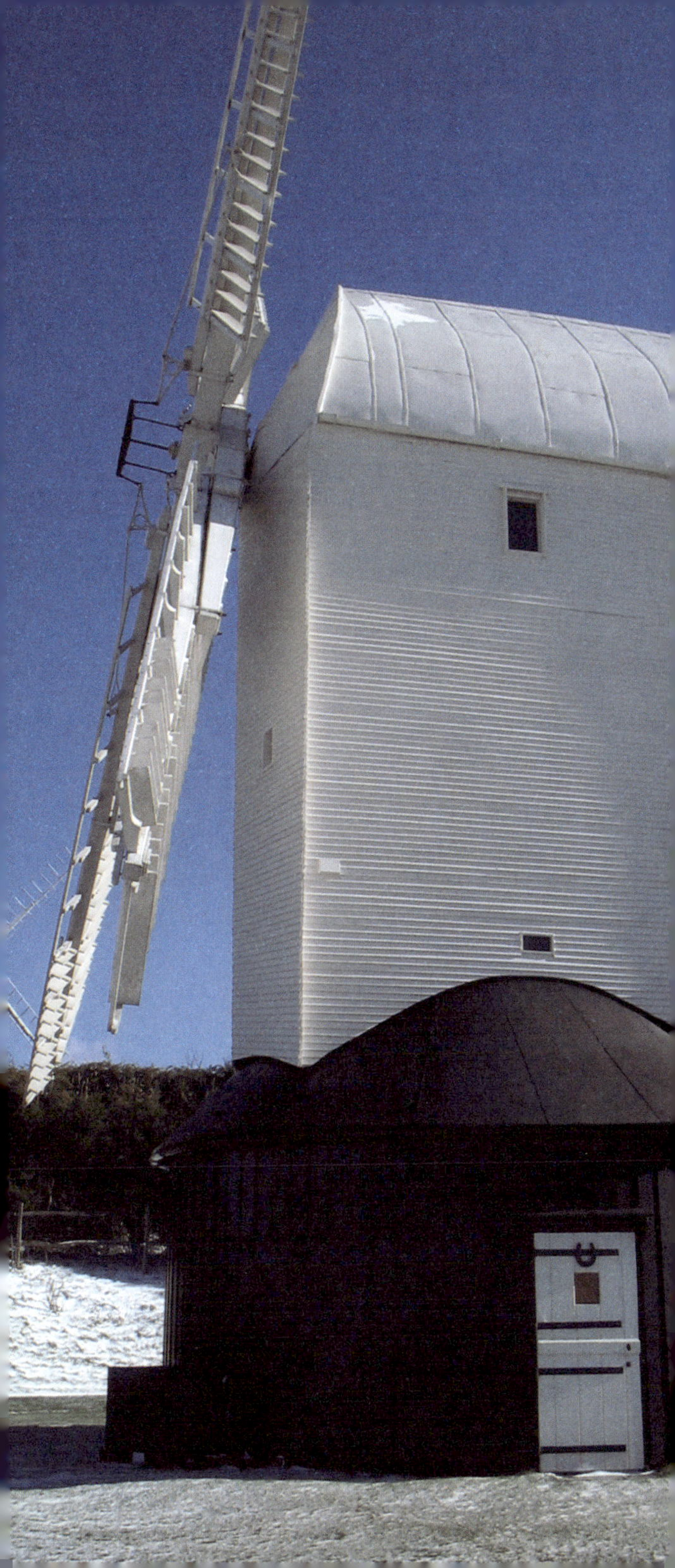

102 Walking

Hove Lagoon to Brighton Marina

Distance: Walk approximately 4 miles (6km)
Time: 3 hours (stopping for lunch)
Start Point: Hove Lagoon

End Point: Black Rock, Brighton Marina
Lunch: Arc, 160 Kings Road Arches (01273) 770505

This lengthy stretch of coastline is actually one of the most accessible walks in Brighton and Hove, following a flat course along the line of the city's beachfront for some three miles.

Built in 1930 as a yachting centre, Hove Lagoon was later used as a military training ground in the run-up to D-Day, with tanks being tested at night to ensure they were watertight. It is actually two lagoons, spanning 10,000sq ft and 210,000sq ft, today used as a model boat lake and a water-sports centre respectively. Permission has also been granted to turn an area to the south into a skate park.

Taking the promenade path eastwards from the lagoon, one of the first buildings you will pass is the eyesore King Alfred Leisure Centre, site of a planned £290 million combined leisure and residential redevelopment by Frank Gehry, architect of Bilbao's iconic Guggenheim Museum.

The views improve as you continue, passing first the ruins of the West Pier, then a series of sandpits, volleyball courts and fish stalls, and finally the bustling bars, cafés and Artists' Quarter beneath Kings Road Arches.

The walk continues past Brighton Pier, either above or below the promenade; along the Volks Railway; and past the nudist beach; before finally culminating at Black Rock on the westernmost edge of the marina.

★ Highlights

Uninterrupted views of English Channel for four miles

Numerous attractions, from Brighton Pier to galleries and bars

0906 711 2255*

103
Walking

Seven Sisters Country Park

Distance: Walk approximately 3 miles (5km)
Time: 2 hrs (round trip, including stop)

Start Point: Seven Sisters Visitor Centre Car park
End Point: Cuckmere Haven
Lunch: Golden Galleon, Exceat Bridge, Seaford (01323) 892247

Named after a succession of seven towering chalk cliffs that stretch along the East Sussex coastline between Seaford and Eastbourne, this largely unspoilt 700-acre beauty spot offers a range of scenic walks.

Drive or catch a number 12 or 13 bus along the coast from Brighton to Seaford, and take a short walk eastwards towards the Golden Galleon pub. Drop down onto the footpath to your right and you will find yourself heading into Seven Sisters Country Park. Between the main road and the seaward horizon, the Cuckmere River snakes southwards towards Cuckmere Haven, flanked by a wide expanse of shimmering shallows.

This beautiful preamble is merely a foretaste of the pleasantries in store as you continue along the three-mile round trip to the sea. The park is a Site of Special Scientific Interest, so bird-watchers should keep an eye out for terns, fulmars and rock pipits, while, on a clear day, watching the sun rise or set over the seven strident cliffs between Haven Brow in the west and Went Hill in the east can be a spectacular experience.

The park also boasts a visitor centre, housed in an 18th-century barn, which is open seven days a week between Easter and October.

★ Highlights
Level, scenic walk to beach following route of Cuckmere River

Visitor centre and museum

*calls cost 50p per minute, UK only

Where to Stay

⭐ Hotels

Drakes Hotel
Awaiting Grading
43-44 Marine Parade
Brighton, BN2 1PE
(01273) 696934

Independently owned Drakes is a unique designled 20-bedroomed hotel on Brighton's seafront. Everything about Drakes is exceptional, from the impeccable service, to the opulent yet serene design and the acclaimed Gingerman restaurant.

Hilton Brighton Metropole
QA Hotel, Kings Road
Brighton, BN1 2FU
(01273) 775432

The 4-star Hilton situated along Brighton's cosmopolitan seafront, guaranteed to make that leisure break that little bit more special.

Starrs Hotel
Awaiting Grading
19 New Steine
Brighton, BN2 1PD
(01273) 607456

A seven-bedroomed hotel, lesbian and gay friendly. Serving full English breakfast. With hotel bar.

⭐ B&B and Guest Houses

Abbey Hotel
★★★
14-19 Norfolk Terrace
Brighton, BN1 3AD
(01273) 724300

3-star Guest Accom rated budget hotel situated in the city centre a few minutes walk from Brighton beach and main shopping centre. Ideally located for all city attractions. Optional continental breakfast and limited parking spaces available.

Adelaide Hotel
★★★★
51 Regency Square
Brighton, BN1 2FF
(01273) 205286

Elegant Regency town house hotel, centrally situated in Brighton's premier seafront square convenient for all amenities, NCP parking and conference venues. No lift.

Ambassador Hotel
♦♦♦♦
22 New Steine
Brighton, BN2 1PD
(01273) 676869

Centrally located in a Georgian garden square overlooking the sea, with 24 en suite rooms, 24-hour reception and security, and residents bar. Green Tourism Scheme 'Gold Award' member. Minutes walk to all main attractions and venues.

Amsterdam Hotel
★★★
11/12 Marine Parade
Brighton, BN2 1TI
(01273) 688825

Hotel with modern, fully equipped rooms, bar and sun terrace. This hotel is suitable for over-18s only – and operates as a gay hotel but everyone is welcome.

Andorra Hotel
♦♦♦
15-16 Oriental Place
Brighton, BN1 2LJ
(01273) 321787

The Andorra Hotel consists of 2 large Regency period houses carefully restored to an excellent standard of comfort and décor.

Atlantic Hotel
★★★
16 Marine Parade
Brighton, BN2 1TL
(01273) 695944

Attractive family-run hotel facing seafront; the Sea Life Centre and Palace Pier, historic Royal Pavilion and famous Lanes are just down the road. Brighton Centre nearby.

Aymer Guest House
♦♦♦♦
13 Aymer Road
Hove, BN3 4GB
(01273) 271165

Delightful Edwardian house close to the seafront and Hove Centre. Convenient for shopping, restaurants and conference venues.

Brighton Kingsway Hotel
♦♦♦♦
2 St. Aubyns
Hove, BN3 2TB
(01273) 722068

17-bedroomed, friendly hotel. Many rooms with sea views and en suite facilities. Close to shops, restaurants and leisure facilities.

brightonwave
♦♦♦♦
10 Madeira Place
Brighton, BN2 1TN
(01273) 676794

4-Diamond Silver accolade hotel, Wi-Fi enabled with 8 luxury en suite rooms all with flat-screen TVs, DVD, and CD players. Centrally located for all shops, bars, restaurants, nightlife and conferences.

Brightside
♦♦♦♦
4 Shirley Road
Hove, BN3 6NN
(01273) 552557

Small friendly bed and breakfast in quiet location with good parking. English country house atmosphere with pretty garden and terrace.

0906 711 2255*

105
Where to Stay

Cavalaire Hotel
◆◆◆◆

34 Upper Rock Gardens
Brighton, BN2 1QF
(01273) 696899

A premier quality guest house offering central location, superior, stylish rooms, excellent customer service, late breakfast and checkout at weekends. Parking available.

C Breeze Hotel
◆◆◆

12a Upper Rock Gardens
Brighton, BN2 1QE
(01273) 602608

Welcoming and charming small hotel. Individually designed en suite rooms. Delicious breakfasts. Eve meals by arrangement. Children and pets welcome. Near the sea and a short walk to the Lanes, conference venues, shopping and restaurants.

Chatsworth Hotel
◆◆

9 Salisbury Road
Hove, BN3 3AB
(01273) 737360

Long-established, well-appointed, quiet, comfortable central Hove hotel. Most rooms have en suite, TV & tea-making facilities. Near County Cricket Ground. Good English cuisine.

Christina Guest House
◆◆◆

20 St. Georges Terrace
Brighton, BN2 1JH
(01273) 690862

Small, friendly house refurbished by new owners. Near Sussex Hospital, Brighton College and seafront. Short walk to the town centre. Freshly cooked Breakfast. Parking possible.

Churchill Guest House
★★★

44 Russell Square
Brighton, BN1 2EF
(01273) 700777

Small friendly guest house overlooking a pleasant garden square in the city centre. All rooms are en suite, with hospitality trays, colour TV and central heating. Price includes full English, continental or vegetarian breakfast.

Claremont House Hotel
◆◆◆◆◆

13 Second Avenue
Hove, Brighton, BN3 2LL
(01273) 735161

Only establishment in city to be awarded VisitBritain's prestigious 5-diamond grading. In quiet conservation area just off the seafront only a short stroll from city-centre shops, attractions, restaurants, bars, clubs and Brighton Centre.

Cosmopolitan Hotel
◆◆◆

29-31 New Steine
Brighton, BN2 1PD
(01273) 682461

The Cosmopolitan is a newly refurbished 39-bedroomed (most en suite) hotel. 18 rooms with sea view located two minutes to seafront and pier. Short walk to town centre. Brand new cocktail bar and separate coffee lounge. 24-hour reception.

Dove Hotel
★★★

18 Regency Square
Brighton, BN1 2FG
(01273) 779222

A beautiful, centrally located, sea front hotel. All rooms are en suite, decorated with taste and care. We offer excellent service, delicious freshly cooked breakfasts and reasonable rates. Full internet access is available.

Funchal Guest House
◆◆◆

17 Madeira Place
Brighton, BN2 1TN
(01273) 603975

Our family-run guesthouse has, for over 40 years, provided excellent breakfasts, cosy rooms, good value for money and is highly recommmended.

Hotel Una
Awaiting Grading

55-56 Regency Square
Brighton, BN1 2FF
(01273) 820464

Hotel accommodation.

Leona House
★★★★

74 Middle Street
Brighton, BN1 1AL
(01273) 327309

4-star 'bijou' Brighton guest accommodation perfectly situated in the heart of the city and just seconds from the famous historic Lanes and Brighton's Conference Centre.

*calls cost 50p per minute, UK only

106 Where to Stay

www.visitbrighton.com

Lichfield House
Awaiting Grading
30 Waterloo Street
Hove, BN3 1AN
(01273) 777740

Listed Regency Townhouse with stylish rooms, just off the seafront. City centre is just a stroll away from this friendly guesthouse. All bedrooms are non-smoking with TV and hospitality tray with 24-hour access. Min 2 nights at weekend.

Maison Mascara Boutique B & B
★★★
33 Montpelier Road
Brighton, BN1 2LQ
(01273) 385959

Centrally located and combining good quality, impeccable cleanliness and professional service. Continental buffet style breakfast only. Free Wi-Fi wireless internet access in most rooms. Stay in style with Maison Mascara.

Marine View
★★★
24 New Steine
Brighton, BN2 1PD
(01273) 603870

Come in, unwind and relax. Enjoy our selection of freshly cooked breakfasts, vegetarian or vegan. Most rooms are en suite. The resident proprietors offer a professional service to ensure that your stay is one to be remembered.

New Madeira Hotel
★★★★
19-23 Marine Parade
Brighton, BN2 1TL
(01273) 698331

On the seafront of this cosmopolitan city's centre with magnificent sea views from a range of well-appointed rooms. 34 comfortable en suite rooms. Located close to Brighton Pier, The Lanes, theatres and restaurants. Friendly staff.

Pavilion Guest House
★★★
12 Madeira Place
Brighton, BN2 1TN
(01273) 683195

Just off the seafront close to all city attractions. All rooms include colour tv, radio alarm, hospitality tray, central heating and access 24 hours with own key. Open all year with a quality English or vegetarian breakfast served daily.

Regency Hotel
Awaiting Grading
28 Regency Square
Brighton
Brighton, BN1 2FH
(01273) 202690

Direct sea views from this Regency townhouse hotel. Restaurants, conference centre and shops nearby. Regency Suite with four-poster bed and balcony. Car park, restaurants, conference centre and shops within 4 minutes walk. Family managed.

Russell Guest House
♦♦♦
19 Russell Square
Brighton, BN1 2EE
(01273) 327969

Family-run guest house situated in a pleasant garden square, minutes from seafront and shopping areas. Access available at all times to enable full enjoyment of the city's evening entertainment. Limited parking available (charge).

Sandpiper Guest House
♦♦♦
11 Russell Square
Brighton, BN1 2EE
(01273) 328202

City-centre location, close to the seafront. All rooms with central heating, colour TV, and coffee/tea facilities. Front rooms with sea views. Internet access on request.

Sea Spray
★★★★
25 New Steine
Brighton, BN2 1PD
(01273) 680332

Stylish boutique hotel with themed rooms and sea views available. Late breakfasts, 'breakfast in bed', veggie/vegan breakfasts all available. Rooms available with internet access, some with CD players and video players.